TRAVEL GUIDE TO THE PEOPLE'S REPUBLIC OF CHINA

TRAVEL GUIDE TO THE PEOPLE'S REPUBLIC OF CHINA

by

Ruth Lor Malloy

WILLIAM MORROW AND COMPANY, INC.
NEW YORK   1975

Photographs: Ruth Lor Malloy
Maps: Dyno Lowenstein

Printed in the United States of America.

1 2 3 4 5 79 78 77 76 75

Library of Congress Cataloging in Publication Data

Malloy, Ruth Lor.
  Travel guide to the People's Republic of China.
  Bibliography: p.
  1. China—Description and travel—1949-   —
Guide-books. I. Title.
DS711.M266 1975   915.1'04'5   75-8510
ISBN 0-688-02933-7

Design: Helen Roberts

ACKNOWLEDGMENTS

In the body of this book are mentioned many people who have shared their experiences in China. But among the unsung contributors—people who also generously shared their knowledge or looked over the manuscript and offered suggestions—I would especially like to mention Dr. Anneliese Gutkind Bulling, William E. Donnett, Betty Rugh Elder, J. M. Fraser, Dr. Kai-yu Hsu, Dr. John Israel, Russell and Irene Johnson, Kenneth and Eleanor Lor, Roy Mah, Esther Mitchell, Edward Neilan, Eunice Riedel, Elliott and Genevieve Nih Schiffmann, Mary Terchek, Dr. Gordon R. Taylor, Ken Woods, Ray Wylie, Dr. and Mrs. Max Zung, and officials of the Overseas Chinese Travel Service in China. Alvin Lee is responsible for most of the Chinese words.

To all of them and especially to my husband, Michael T. Malloy, who made my own trip possible and helped with editing and baby-sitting, I hope future China travelers will be grateful. I know I am.

CONTENTS

CONTENTS

CONTENTS

CONTENTS

xiii

INTRODUCTION

Visiting China is like visiting nowhere else in the world. It is more personal than other countries. Visitors are honored guests as proud Chinese hosts bustle about trying to give favorable impressions, pleased you have come.

China is not interested in large-scale, commercial tourism. It prefers to provide "Responsible Persons" to care for guests, protecting you from inconveniences. It is unhappy about letting you wander around entirely by yourselves, perhaps missing what China wants to show you.

Except for visitors to the Canton Trade Fair, this approach means at least one Responsible Person per visitor or group of visitors. With a limited number of Responsible Persons available, it is easy to see why China prefers groups.

If it wanted to, China could build more hotels and train more interpreters and guides to meet the wishes of everyone willing and able to go there—but it does not want to. Outside influences could get out of hand, and China is too busy raising the living standards of all its people and maintaining the purity of its revolutionary ideals to add to its problems.

This guide is an expanded version of my first book, *A Guide to the People's Republic of China for Travelers of Chinese Ancestry*. It is based on interviews with China visitors from many countries, and on my own visits to China in 1965 and 1973, as an Overseas Chinese journalist.

The information here should help *all* foreigners interested in visiting China. It tells how most people got their visas and what they saw and did when they got there. If you are lucky enough to get a visa, what you will see and do will be basically the same; everyone visits communes, factories, and schools; and most visit the Great Wall and the Forbidden City.

There will be some differences in detail, however, because China is in a state of flux, constantly evaluating and changing its policies in regard to visitors. Nothing is stable in a continuing revolution. Let me know how your experiences differ.

Because I am fond of China and because I think China has a lot to offer the rest of the world and vice versa, I write in the hope that this book will help you plan your trip successfully, and that your visit will be mutually beneficial.

RUTH LOR MALLOY

TRAVEL GUIDE TO THE PEOPLE'S REPUBLIC OF CHINA

The People's Republic of China

1
Before You Even Start— How Badly Do You Want to Go?

NOT FOR THE HEDONIST

China has no night clubs, no call girls, no foreign movies, and no escapist television. In 1975 all the neon signs said "Long Live Chairman Mao," and all visitors go the commune-school-factory route. Your hotel probably will not be air-conditioned in the summer, nor will some of the buildings you visit be heated in the cold of winter.

If being luxuriously entertained is your thing, then China is not for you.

SOME MAY NEED COURAGE

China is a Communist country, for many years an "enemy" to some parts of the world. In some countries, this atmosphere of suspicion still persists. So do consider whether going will jeopardize your job; will the police check up on you—and do you care? A handful out of the thousands of Chinese-American visitors were politely interviewed by the FBI about their post-Nixon visits. Some South Africans have managed to go to China, entering via Macao where somehow their passports weren't stamped. If your country still considers China an enemy, you may have to be equally resourceful.

HOW SAFE IS IT?

I feel that visas for China are so rare that, if you have one, you should use it. It may be the only opportunity you will have to go, and your chances of unpleasant incidents are greater in New York City or Rome.

You may have read about violence in China—campaigns against Lin Piao and Confucius, and the Cultural Revolution. Even war with Russia is a possibility. But generally speaking, I think it is safe if China grants you a visa.

The Chinese are conscientious hosts. If there is any chance of danger, your visa will be cancelled, or you won't be allowed to visit questionable areas.

Unpleasant incidents happen usually to foreign residents who are not under the care of a Responsible Person or to foreigners who neglect to ask permission to take a photo of an individual or a "Big Character Poster."

ARE VISITORS BRAINWASHED?

Tours in China are usually two or three weeks long. If you're worried about a dramatic change in your values in so little time, your judgment system must be pretty weak to begin with.

Yes, you will be propagandized; you will be shown one point of view—the party line. But it is "soft sell," not a hard-driving, systematic attempt to convince you China is right. Brainwashing, like psychotherapy, is a long-term, well-calculated process. It needs time and isolation to work—so you won't get it.

To safeguard your objectivity, read both sides of the China question before and after you go. You will probably not be able to talk to anyone in China itself who will criticize the government or the way of life. But do not be afraid to ask frank questions of the people you meet.

A trip to China can be an intellectual and spiritual challenge. If you are upset by ideas different from your own, don't go.

NOT FOR THE LAZY

Two or three weeks in China is usually packed full of things to do morning, afternoon, and some evenings, especially if you are part of a tour group. While your hosts are very considerate of elderly and disabled people, the able-bodied will be expected to tour indefatigably—though the Chinese will understand if you want to take the afternoon off. You do get a two-hour lunch break! So get into shape and come on!

3

2
That Elusive Visa

IF AT FIRST . . .

I get the impression that the number of people allowed to visit China from any one country depends not on the number who apply, but on China's current policy toward that country, the number of hotel rooms and interpreters and plane seats available, and on whether China is going through one of its periodic political struggles.

Getting a visa also depends on your reasons for going; mere sight-seeing isn't enough. Persons seriously interested in China's development have a good chance at the few visas available; so have persons of Chinese ancestry bent on seeing relatives and/or the changes since they or their ancestors left China. Then there are the technical and cultural missions invited as a result of government agreements.

All visa applications are decided in Peking, so don't bother flirting with the consul in Ottawa or Tokyo. Try concentrating on that computer mastermind in Peking. Luck and timing also have a lot to do with it. In 1971, the U.S. table tennis team made no formal request to visit China—just a remark to a member of the Chinese team during an international tournament in Tokyo.

"Why shouldn't the American team be permitted to come?" asked Chairman Mao Tsetung when he heard of it—or so Harrison Salisbury relates the story. And the team was invited.

On the other hand, Salisbury himself, who is an editor of *The New York Times,* tells about trying a couple of times a year since 1949 to get permission to visit China. He never received a direct answer to any of his communications to Premier Chou En-lai, but he did get to go after twenty years of trying.

So be persistent; it will show your serious interest. If you get no reply to your first overtures, try again in six months, and then six months after that. At least you'll be in line if and when China does open her door to foreigners in larger numbers.

The methods listed here do not guarantee you a visa, but if you use them, you improve your chances of getting one.

STANDARD PROCEDURE—BUT DO READ ON

First, contact a Chinese diplomatic mission and ask what the current procedure is to get a visa. I suggest you telephone if you can; you may not get a reply to your letter. Don't give up if the person who answers the phone tries to discourage you.

The mission will probably either tell you to write a

letter of application to the mission, or directly to *Luxingshe,* the China International Travel Service in Peking. If you write to Peking, also send a carbon copy to the mission.

WRITING FOR PERMISSION TO APPLY FOR A VISA

The letter should ask for *permission to apply* for a visa—or visas, if you are going with a group. Information should include name, nationality, sex, occupation, a short biography, languages spoken, reason for going, dates, and places you wish to visit. Some successful applicants have written two paragraphs, others elevenpage biographies. Include anything you think will show the sincerity of your desire. If you are of Chinese ancestry, or were born in China, or have worked with Chou En-lai—say so. Keep a copy of your letter for your own reference.

Purpose:

Since a clear statement of purpose is very important, let me mention again that you will get nowhere if you say you just want to sight-see. If it applies, retired persons should say they want to study the aged and retirement in China; factory workers could mention studying the living and working conditions of their Chinese counterparts; American blacks could be interested in China's treatment of her ethnic minorities; California farmers might want to look at China's irrigation methods.

Politicians could mention wanting to study how China got rid of its drug addiction problem, unemployment, and inflation. Government administrators might want to look into the treatment of the mentally ill, care for the indigent, law and order, flood control, city planning, and public services.

In writing about your purpose, back up your statements with evidence of genuine interest in old people, or minorities, or irrigation or whatever, by mentioning your research in the field, publications on the subject, work experience, or personal background.

Read about how things are done in your field of interest in China and show some knowledge of them in your letter.

But do not flatter; the Chinese are good at spotting phonies.

Group or Alone?

As for going as *a group or alone*—unless you are a VIP or Overseas Chinese or a special case, or unless some clerk makes a mistake, your chances of going to China alone are very slim.

And the group route isn't easy.

Groups can run from four to twenty-five—usually ten to twenty. You could contact your professional society, union, or anything else you belong to and ask if it is organizing a trip to China that you could join. One neighborhood in New York City wrote to Peking saying something like, "Look here. So far, only important people have been allowed to visit China. How about a group of us ordinary people?" They were given visas.

You could try to organize a group yourself, but be prepared for a great deal of frustration as people you count on drop out, or are late in handing in their documents—and then the Chinese themselves say "no."

7

Because of the time span between the first application and the actual trip, the Chinese do understand that substitutions have to be made.

The Centre for Continuing Education of the University of British Columbia organized a tour by Canadian women in 1973. "We were not given 'blanket approval' for the people selected for the tour," says MaryFrank Macfarlane, Director of the Language Institute there. "However, the individuals were quite carefully selected by us and all names submitted were approved."

In the past, China has received many groups, among them high school students, farmers (called "peasants" in China), workers, medical practitioners, political activists, and members of ethnic minorities. My guess is that less than half of these were Communists or even sympathizers.

Itinerary:

In planning your itinerary, take into account the weather and vastness of China. If you want to see a lot of countryside, ask to go part of the way by train; but also consider that even by train it takes about twenty-four hours to go from Peking to Shanghai and a little more than a day from Shanghai to Canton. Luxingshe does have a list of tours you can choose from. One typical 21-day tour included Canton, Peking, Shihchiachuang, Nanking, Shanghai, and Hangchow. A 28-day trip included Canton, Peking, Sian, Shanghai, and Hangchow. (See the section on Sample Prices in Chapter 15.)

Chapter 12 lists cities that foreigners have recently been allowed to visit. You could ask for places not listed there, but you will be extremely lucky if you are allowed to go. I have heard of only three or four foreigners being allowed to visit Szechuan province, one or two being allowed into Sinkiang, Tibet, or Inner Mongolia.

The Best Time to Go:

It is chilly in the winter in **Canton**. This shouldn't bother Canadians like me, said one helpful official, but he admitted there was no heat in the Overseas Chinese Hotel. You need a top coat and a heavy sweater into April. In April and May there is a lot of rain, so a very light plastic raincoat or an umbrella is essential. The summer is very hot and there is air-conditioning in only a few buildings. The best time to visit is late September and October, or April and May, if you can take the humidity.

The best time to visit **Peking** is in the autumn, since summers are hot, winters are cold, and the spring has a dry wind blowing dust in from the hills to the north. Peking is almost the same latitude as Philadelphia. If you are not in a hurry to get things done, a good time to visit is around the May 1 (if you can take the dust) and October 1 holidays. Special arrangements are made to have foreign guests attend holiday functions, but any other special requests or tours have to wait until institutions and schools open again.

The best time to visit **Shanghai** is March to May, or September to November. Summers there have a 38° C (100° F) maximum and winters have a minus 10° C (14° F) minimum.

Unless you have a special interest in them, I advise avoiding the Canton Trade Fairs since facilities, especially in Canton, are most crowded then. (See Chapter 15 for dates.)

9

Should You Take Your Children?

I took my five-year-old with me for a five-week visit in 1973 and I was glad I did. I did not use a baby-sitter because I found I could take her with me to movies and theatrical performances in the evenings. Chinese dance dramas are easy for a child to understand and the acrobats are fun for all ages. At the communes and factories, somehow there was always a helpful hand around to amuse her while the grown-ups talked. The Chinese love children.

She especially had a ball visiting friends and relatives. There were always piles of other children around, and it took her only about ten minutes to be arm in arm with them.

My daughter could only count in Chinese when she arrived, but even this helped because all school-age children can count in Peking dialect and she would make a game of it.

People on the street and in buses would stop and try to talk to her. Because she is a flirt, barriers of formality melted right away, and I think on one occasion we even got a room in an overcrowded hotel because of her.

You can get milk in the big cities, usually served hot with sugar. When we went to a small city, we took Australian "Long Life" milk in cartons, bought in Hong Kong. It tasted almost like milk from home without mixing with water. No refrigeration is needed until opened, but the cartons are bulky.

You can buy powdered and evaporated milk in China, but they are expensive and the powdered milk does not mix easily with the hot water usually available for drinking. One does not drink tap water in China.

I didn't find a hot dog or a hamburger, but if your child is unhappy without these the International Club in Peking or the Seamen's Club in Shanghai might have them.

Transportation costs for children under two, not occupying a seat, are 10 percent of adult fares; from two to twelve, half fare.

Translating Your Letter into Chinese:

It is not necessary to have your letter of application translated into Chinese, but if you do, it is a courtesy —and I feel that you have a better chance of getting results. The Chinese get thousands of letters like yours each year, and they are short of translators. I suspect many letters end up in waste baskets.

If you can't do the job yourself, getting a translator may be expensive. You are lucky if you have a Chinese friend who can do it for you. Don't worry if he does not know the modernized characters used in China today. Many of the older officials will understand the old characters and might even be pleased at your thoughtfulness as long as your friend doesn't insult China by using Confucian phrases and archaic place names (such as calling Peking "Peiping").

If you are a perfectionist, you could pay a translator up to fifty dollars a page to get your letter perfect in the modern idiom. (See Chapter 16.)

When you send your letter to the Chinese, be sure to send both the English version and the translation. If there is a translation error, the English can be referred to.

If you get a reply, asking for more information, then feel optimistic. The Chinese frequently do not answer letters unless there is something positive to say. It may still take over a month, however, before you get an acknowledgment to your second letter. Then another wait of perhaps four more months as your application is processed in Peking.

YOUR VISA APPLICATION

When you get a reply giving you permission to apply for a visa, it may still take another month before you can go. You will then be asked for two photographs, a fee (in 1974 it came to six dollars in American currency), and a completed application form.

The form will also ask: name, nationality, sex, date of birth, place of birth, marital status, religion, and political party; kind of passport and number, date and authority of issue, and expiration date; present occupation and place of work, and present address.

The form will also ask: Been in service of what institutions? When? Where and what work undertaken? Accompanying family members (name, sex, age, nationality, and relationship to applicant). Object of journey to China. Itinerary and means of transportation, dates, port of entry into China and means, port of departure. Sources of livelihood in China. Previous visits to China. Closest relatives and friends in China.

The application concludes with a pledge for self-support in all the expenses incurred in China.

You may have mentioned most of these items before in your earlier letters. Never mind. Give them again.

THE CHINA TRAVEL SERVICE, HONG KONG

This is only an agent for the Chinese government travel services and does not make decisions on visa applications. In 1973, a clerk there said it prefers that all applications be made through the Chinese diplomatic missions abroad. But I have heard that some people since then have been able to get permission from this office to enter China. So try, if you are in the area. But do not count on getting permission during a short visit to Hong Kong (see Chapter 5). It can take six months or a couple of years unless you have an invitation from a Chinese organization already in hand.

Permission for Overseas Chinese to Enter China:

For Overseas Chinese (i.e., persons of Chinese ancestry with non-Chinese passports), permission *to enter* China may be more readily granted than to Foreign Friends (i.e., visitors who are not of Chinese ancestry). But make sure you know what you're getting. "Permission to enter China" means only that. It is not a visa. It does not mean permission *to leave.*

While I have heard of no one being detained in China, getting permission to leave China necessitates another application and a wait of from one to seven days in the last city visited in China. The delay may be annoying and inconvenient. Persons with visas do not have this problem.

Another disadvantage is that only persons with valid visas can enter Friendship Stores and the International Club in Peking.

13

See also the last section of this chapter and Chapter 7.

Hong Kong Residents:

Persons with Hong Kong identity papers and permission to reenter Hong Kong, which is a British colony, can easily get permission to travel in China. They should also go to the China Travel Service to make travel arrangements or just show up at the Kowloon train station.

WRITING TO OTHER ORGANIZATIONS IN CHINA

Some foreigners have contacted the Chinese organizations related to their fields of interest and have received invitations to visit China, which made them eligible for visas.

For example, the All-China Sports Federation has issued invitations to athletes. Individual journalists should write to the Information Department, Ministry of Foreign Affairs, Peking. Some journalistic groups have been hosted by *Hsinhua*, the New China News Agency. Nongovernment VIPs should write to the Chinese People's Association for Friendship with Foreign Countries or the People's Institute for Foreign Affairs.

If you qualify, just write to these organizations in Peking, no street address necessary.

SCHOLARS

You may be aware of agreements by your government and China's for exchanges of scholars. Some governments have set up or appointed organizations to work out these exchanges. In the United States there is the Committee on Scholarly Communication with the People's Republic of China, which is made up of the American Council of Learned Societies, the National Academy of Sciences, and the Social Science Research Council.

In Canada, check with the East Asia Division, Department of External Affairs, Ottawa.

Write to these organizations if you think you qualify. One advantage is that your expenses will be paid. But if it's a holiday you're interested in, better not go this route. Scholars spend most of their time on visits to research institutes, universities, laboratories, hospitals, factories, and communes. They hold seminars with Chinese scholars and give lectures.

Even if you cannot be included in an official exchange, you can still apply to the Chinese diplomatic mission in your country, or directly to an organization in China. Names of research institutes can be found in Chinese scholarly journals, and your letters can be addressed to them, c/o the Chinese Academy of Sciences (Academia Sinica). Medical personnel should write to the Chinese Medical Association, c/o Academia Sinica.

Scholars can write to either the Foreign Affairs Department of the Chinese Academy of Sciences or the Foreign Affairs Department of the Scientific and Technical Association, since it seems both foreign affairs departments are actually one and the same.

Again your letter should include a *curriculum vitae,* a description of the institutions you are affiliated with, a list of your publications, and a detailed description of what you want to do in China.

In the United States, the Committee on Scholarly Communication publishes a newsletter three or four times a year, listing its exchanges and scholars who have made the trip. It also gives up-to-date advice on how to contact the Chinese, news about scientific journals and resource materials, and bibliographies of articles and books by travelers to China.

During 1971–72, approximately one hundred American scholars visited China. If you have friends who are going, ask them to recommend you for an invitation, which also might work.

BUSINESS PEOPLE

Business people are in a class by themselves. One of the best methods of negotiating business contracts with China is by attending the Chinese Export Commodities Fair (also known as the Canton or Kwangchow Trade Fair).

For general information, consult the commerce department of your own country. It may even publish a guide on how to trade with China. If you are in Hong Kong, you can consult your country's mission there, an international bank like the Bank of America, or the Hongkong and Shanghai Banking Corporation. The Chinese General Chamber of Commerce is also supposed to be helpful. Americans can contact the American Chamber of Commerce of Hong Kong.

On specific matters, you should contact the Chinese state trading corporation dealing with the kind of merchandise you wish to buy or sell. The addresses are in Chapter 16. If you cannot decide which corporation can help you, write to the Chinese Council for the Promotion of International Trade in Peking, and it should forward your letter. If China is interested, the corporation will issue you an invitation to the Trade Fair. This invitation will entitle you to receive a visa, sometimes within a day at a Chinese mission if your representative can personally fill out the visa application forms. It is possible to do this by post or at the China Travel Service in Hong Kong, but these will take longer. Plan on four business days for the Hong Kong pick-up.

In the United States, there is the National Council for U.S.-China Trade, which describes itself as a "private, nonprofit corporation committed to facilitate the development of U.S. trade and commercial relations with the People's Republic of China." Its member firms include the Coca-Cola Export Corporation, Bulova Watch Company, Bank of America, and United Air Lines. David Rockefeller is a Vice-Chairman.

The National Council publishes a handbook for U.S. businessmen to the Canton Trade Fair and a helpful sixty-dollars-a-year magazine, *U.S. China Business Review.*

China Consultants International, Limited, in addition to helping businessmen trade with China, publishes *American Industrial Report* six times a year, in cooperation with the National Council. With a circulation of 15,000, this Chinese-language magazine is sent to purchasing officials in China, i.e., "engineers, teachers, commune leaders, factory managers and workers in a position to place requirements on the foreign trade corporations."

There are some opportunities for Trade Fair visitors to see Canton and even other parts of China. In the lobbies of the hotels used by Trade Fair visitors, the Fair organizers post notices for tours on Sundays and holidays, to communes and factories, and tickets for cultural and sports events.

Visitors are also free to take any form of public transportation to most places in Canton, but to travel outside of Canton they must get permission from a Trade Fair liaison office, or the Overseas Chinese Travel Service. Maps of Canton showing major scenic attractions and points of interest are available in English at the hotels and the Fair.

A few businessmen travel to Shanghai and Peking to visit factories manufacturing the products they are interested in buying. Sometimes they go to discuss business directly with the Trading Corporations, which frequently arrange trips to local scenic attractions as well as factories and industrial exhibits.

THE TRAVEL AGENCY WAY

Some Canadian and American travel agencies have offered tours and help to get visas, but few have succeeded in giving tours of China except to Overseas Chinese. One agency said it stopped trying to organize China tours because "they cost too much." Another agency said they were booked a year in advance.

A couple of agencies that have the reputation for successfully booking tours are listed in Chapter 16. If you are interested, write to see if you qualify. Some of these arrange tours for persons of similar backgrounds, like workers or doctors or teachers.

IF YOU'RE EXCEPTIONALLY LUCKY

Sometimes ordinary tourists intent on good times rather than revolutionary lectures have been admitted to

China. In 1973, over 350 passengers from the S.S. *France,* on a round-the-world cruise, were able to take a train from Hong Kong to Canton for about four days. A British liner stopped over in Tientsin and Shanghai that same year and, in 1974, passengers from a Dutch liner also spent three days in Canton. If you're interested, do read Richard Joseph's enthusiastic account of the visit of passengers of the S.S. *Veendam* in the August 1974 issue of *Esquire.*

Lucky, too, are those who are invited along for a week in China on an inaugural flight of an airline going there. But you really need more than a few days to absorb what is going on.

Some have gone in the entourage of a VIP like actress Shirley MacLaine, or were invited as a member of a radical racial minority that China wanted to encourage.

Some spouses are lucky if they can tag along when their mates receive visas. Overseas Chinese can take along a non-Chinese spouse at the cheaper Overseas Chinese rates. Some scientists (Tuzo Wilson, for instance) have taken their wives, but the Committee on Scholarly Communication won't let its exchange scholars do this.

I know one couple who got a visa in 1971 because of an invitation from a very important resident of China, Prince Sihanouk of Cambodia—and an Overseas Chinese from Canada got permission because he knew an important Communist leader in Hong Kong.

Even members of national China friendship associations—like the U.S.-China Friendship Association and the Canada-China Friendship Association—need luck to go to China. There are so few places for the many who want to go. In 1974, there were friendship associations in twenty-eight U.S. cities.

A few activists of the associations are given all-expense paid trips to China from Hong Kong. The organizations can recommend people of notable influence to be invited by China, usually at the traveler's expense. It is hoped that all these people will publicize their visits on their return.

If you are interested, look for the association in your local phone book. Failing that, you can write for the address of the closest association to you from one of the addresses in Chapter 16. These associations are interested in promoting friendship. They organize lectures, slide shows, and movies on China, and tend to be left-wing. If your city doesn't have one, you may want to start a local group yourself.

The *Guardian Radical News Weekly,* described by one observer as "more left than Mao," has organized over a dozen group tours, usually at the expense of the traveler. Read actress Candice Bergen's account of one in *Playboy* magazine before you apply for one of these.

OLD CHINA HANDS

For foreigners who have lived and worked in pre-revolutionary China, and for their China-born children, I can only pass on the experiences of an American friend who was born and raised in a provincial capital in central China, where her parents were associated with an American-sponsored school and hospital, a generation ago.

"In June 1973, I went to the China Travel Service in Hong Kong, telling them I wanted to visit my birthplace and study the state of nursing in China. I said I would only be in Hong Kong until January 1974.

20

"They told me to write to Luxingshe in Peking, which I did immediately, making a very simple itinerary, and asking only to go by train to Canton and thence to my birthplace, an overnight train ride away.

"I asked to visit my old home, a national monument nearby, and several medical facilities since I am a nurse. I also said I wanted to see the changes that had occurred as I knew things had improved a lot since before Liberation. I had left China when I was fourteen, twenty-five years before.

"I apologized for not requesting to visit more renowned places, saying that it was not through lack of desire, but rather to spend the little time available for the purposes stated. I asked for two to three weeks. I also said I was studying Mandarin.

"I received no reply all summer. In October, I went back to the China Travel Service in Hong Kong and, while waiting, heard the clerk turn away an Asian scholar from some U.S. university. I told them I had received no reply. They asked again why I wanted to go—so I said I really just wanted to visit my home town. Much to my flabbergastation, they said they thought I had a chance and suggested I apply for December, writing a second letter. I said that I would have to take the children if we went in December because my husband would not be able to take care of them at that time. They said 'go ahead' so I wrote again, giving biographies of the two girls and the reason I had to take them.

"Four weeks to the day, I got a reply, giving permission not just for the three of us, but also for my husband. Because of the additional cost, we could only spend a week there. It cost us U.S. $40 per adult per day, and half price per child.

"Should foreigners who had been expelled try to

21

visit? My father was tried, imprisoned, and forced to leave shortly after Liberation. I don't think he should go back."

Her experiences in China are related in Chapter 13.

TEACHERS OF A FOREIGN LANGUAGE

Foreigners have been able to work in China on one- or two-year contracts, teaching a language at the Foreign Languages Institutes in some Chinese cities. Teachers usually live in school housing with other foreign teachers, or in hotels, and are paid a modest stipend based on education and experience. They also get free accommodations, medical treatment, summer travel, and other privileges.

Recently Chinese students were sent to England for language training, so there may not be as much demand now for foreign teachers, but do try if you are interested. The situation keeps changing. In 1965, the languages taught included Russian, French, German, Spanish, Japanese, Arabic, and English. Shanghai had about forty foreign teachers and Peking about one hundred. Other universities also have foreign language departments.

Canadian Ray Wylie taught in Shanghai in 1965 and 1966. He first applied in March 1965 at a Chinese embassy and was offered the job officially five months later. He feels he was accepted because he had the appropriate education (B.A. in History), was young and adaptable, and was fairly left-wing politically, though not a Marxist-Leninist.

In China, he received 380 yuan (about U.S.$190) a month and was able to save money because of the lower cost of living. He had complete freedom to travel within a ten-mile radius of Shanghai. Usually it took a few days to get permission to go elsewhere, but he was able to visit towns, factories, and communes not usually open to foreign visitors. He was often allowed to travel without an escort.

Mr. Wylie found the experience very satisfactory in spite of frustrations such as limited personal contact with Chinese colleagues and students, and his own limited knowledge of Chinese.

For anyone interested in applying for a teaching position, Mr. Wylie suggests contacting the nearest Chinese embassy, the Committee for Cultural Relations with Foreign Countries in Peking, and/or the nearest national China friendship society.

AS A STUDENT

Some Overseas Chinese have studied at universities in China, the arrangements made during a trip to China. There are also student exchanges arranged between China and other governments such as Canada. *Parade* magazine reported that Yale University is hoping to send two students a year to study Chinese and perhaps teach English at the high school and college levels.

Here, too, you should enquire at a Chinese embassy, the Committee for Cultural Relations with Foreign Countries in Peking, and/or the nearest national China friendship society.

And be sure to read John Burns' two articles in the Toronto *Globe and Mail* on Canadian students in Peking. See Bibliography.

THE OVERSEAS CHINESE

(See also Chapter 7.) Persons of Chinese ancestry are, in a way, the most privileged of the ordinary China visitors. We are under the wing of the Overseas Chinese Travel Service rather than Luxingshe (which takes care of most Foreign Friends). It is a completely different category with different rules.

We have a better chance of getting visas. We are treated as visiting family, given freedom to travel without escort to see relatives and ancestral homes even in areas not usually accessible to foreigners. We can also import free of duty into China, as gifts to friends and relatives, a long list of things including a watch, a radio, a sewing machine (better make it a treadle), a camera, a bicycle (most in China are black), and 120 yards of cotton textiles (conservative colors for adults). I found some of these items were cheaper in Hong Kong, even though they were made in China. Relatives told me it was difficult to get even locally made bicycles and sewing machines in China.

Accommodations can be cheaper than for Foreign Friends; and we have a better chance of staying longer, studying at universities, getting long-term medical treatment, and staying with friends or relatives.

On the other hand, the customs search for Overseas Chinese at the border is much more thorough. Frequently Foreign Friends are not searched at all. I had four customs officials going through my bags, poking even into my Band-Aid boxes.

And the Overseas Chinese hotels are not as classy. Unless we opt for a group tour around China, we usually have to wait four days for permission to go to cities not listed on our visas, and several days for plane tickets. If we stay with relatives, we have to register with the authorities at each place we visit, and enroll ourselves at the local ration office for grain ration coupons.

But as far as I can tell, the only real disadvantage is language. If you don't speak Chinese, the Overseas Chinese Travel Service has very few English-speaking Responsible Persons to help you.

What Is an Overseas Chinese?

When I first applied to travel to China in 1965, I asked the China Travel Service in Hong Kong this question.

The man answered, "It is not where your parents come from that makes you Overseas Chinese; it is how you feel that makes you Overseas Chinese."

On my 1973 visit, I did not get this impression at all. An official of the Overseas Chinese Travel Service in Canton told me anyone with Chinese blood was Overseas Chinese. This included my five-year-old daughter whose father is a Latvian-Irish American. She doesn't feel anything in particular.

Did my Overseas Chinese status mean that China has a claim on me? So far, I have found no evidence of this. China has frequently urged persons of Chinese origin to be good citizens of the country in which they live. I have never been asked to do anything for China.

Are You Worried About Going?

Many persons of Chinese ancestry wonder if they will be detained if they visit, but every year, thousands of Overseas Chinese visit and leave China. They come from all over the world, mainly Southeast Asia. Some were born in China but have resident status in other countries. Some are citizens of other countries.

I checked with both the Canadian and United States governments and found that as far as knowledgeable officials knew, not one of their citizens of Chinese origin had ever been detained in China. Canadians have been visiting the People's Republic since Liberation; Americans since 1971.

China at the moment is encouraging Overseas Chinese visitors. No one would want to go there if visitors were held against their will. No one would go if they knew they would be followed. I doubt that China has the huge intelligence network that would be needed to shadow the thousands of Overseas Chinese visitors in Canton alone!

I must relate here what happened to a Chinese-American scholar who spent five and a half months in China collecting material and interviewing people for a book. He wrote, "Three days before we left China, a party from the Public Security office seized all my photographs, notes, and books, which have never been recovered. A spokesman told us, 'It is clear by evidence obtained, that under the cover of visiting relatives, you, an American of Chinese extraction, have been conducting illegal activities of gathering information for the purpose of espionage and sabotage.' "

My friend was not detained, but escorted politely out of the country.

Some Overseas Chinese are afraid that their visit may bring trouble to their Chinese relatives. I found that during the Cultural Revolution and during periods of economic difficulties, yes, there were some hardships for persons in contact with relatives abroad. When there were food shortages in the country, rice rations were cut even more, for instance, for those believed to be getting extra money from overseas.

But in 1973, relatives and friends in China assured me there was no trouble; no one would harass them with questions because I visited them. In 1965, before the Cultural Revolution, I wrote about some of my relatives in a national Canadian magazine, and even these said no one bothered them as a result.

People I met gave me names and addresses of relatives in America to look up. "Would I come here to the hotel to meet you if I were afraid?" one friend assured me.

Another friend did say he was afraid to meet me at the hotel. It wasn't because he would be annoyed by questions *after* the visit; it was because he had to make application *before* going into the hotel, giving his name, address, age, and I.D. number as well as my name and my relationship to him and why he wanted to see me. He was nervous about answering that kind of question, even though the visit itself, he assured me, would have no repercussions.

China, however, has gone through several periods of anti-foreign feelings. The best guide is to write to your friends and relatives and ask if they want you to look them up.

Some Overseas Chinese wonder if their relatives will ask for money or help. This depends on your relatives. A Chinese businessman from Singapore told me his sister in Shanghai had a very good job and gave him back the clothes he brought her as a present. She said she didn't need them and that she had asked for a reduction in her salary because she didn't need so much money.

Other people found their relatives asking for used clothing, but used clothing can no longer be mailed in.

27

They also asked for money and medicines; jobs and spouses for relatives already abroad; and help in leaving China.

At the moment, permission to leave China and join families abroad is very difficult to obtain, but it is not impossible for some people. Canada and China have an agreement to allow some Chinese citizens to join their families in Canada. Canadian immigration officials started to process visas to Canada in Canton in 1974. Check with your country's diplomatic mission in Peking. The Canadian embassy, for example, told me application has to be made first in Canada. Once that is approved, then permission from the Chinese government can be applied for. It is a long process.

Language Problems:

The Overseas Chinese Travel Service suggested that persons with no Chinese whatsoever had better travel as Foreign Friends, like other foreigners. In 1973, I did not meet any English-speaking Responsible Person in Canton, but one of the two in Shanghai did help me. In Peking, there were only two, but these were too busy to take me around.

You could take a chance that you will meet some bilingual Overseas Chinese who will help you. Tour guides usually speak the Peking dialect, and if you only speak Cantonese, you may have a problem.

I don't speak much Chinese but found it possible to have a good time, even without an interpreter. The Chinese try very hard to understand. Sometimes I found other English-speaking guests to help if I had something vital to say. I had a dictionary handy, drew pictures, and tried charades. I also had a set of helpful phrases written in Chinese, which usually worked.

I enjoyed looking for English-speaking guests. American and Canadian Chinese usually look more prosperous than those from other countries. The men, especially the Americans, have a look of individuality and usually wear leather shoes instead of cloth or plastic, especially in Canton. They wear colored knit or polyester shirts rather than nylon or Dacron, and their suits have less sheen. Some Singapore, Hong Kong, Japanese, and Malayan Chinese also speak good English and it was interesting to meet them.

Must You Go on a Group Tour?

Overseas Chinese can usually apply to enter China alone. You do this at a Chinese mission rather than by writing to Peking. When you arrive in China, you may have to join a tour group to see the country. This will depend on how crowded the travel facilities are. If you arrive in Canton during the Trade Fair, you may not have any other choice. But if you arrive first in Peking or Shanghai, you may not get to join one since the groups are usually made up in Canton.

There are advantages to a group tour. They can be a little cheaper than traveling alone, and a guide will take care of the bureaucratic details. And you can avoid many delays because your group is expected for dinner, for example, at a specific time. Food and tables will be ready. The individual traveler may have to wait as long as two hours for lunch.

You may also be able to visit factories and hospitals you cannot visit as an individual, and have the opportunity to ask questions of knowledgeable officials.

29

Of course there are also disadvantages. You may want to go to some but not all the places on your tour. I met a Chinese-American anesthetist who entered China alone, joined a tour, and was not able to see the thing he was most interested in—acupuncture anesthesia. No one else in his group was interested and nothing could be arranged for one person at that time.

There is also the possibility of having to wait in Canton for a week or two before a group is organized. They go whenever there are about twenty-five people. And of course you may find some incompatible people in your group—chronic late-comers who hold you up—it happens everywhere. But you will find pleasant and helpful people as well.

As a group, you will be looked on as a curiosity by local Chinese. As an individual, you might have a chance to approach them and make friends. I was taken home by a man I met in a park once, but I don't think it would have happened if I were in a group. And you might get tired of visiting all those factories, communes, and schools.

Some people have been able to leave their groups to visit relatives and friends in some of the cities on their itinerary. Of course, there is always the possibility of going alone to see relatives before or after the tour.

You may want to organize your own group before you visit China, to insure that you see just exactly what you want, and to insure that you get an English- or Cantonese-speaking guide if you don't understand Peking dialect. Write to the Overseas Chinese Travel Service in Canton, or in the China Travel Building, 77, Queen's Road, Central, Hong Kong.

3
When You See the Light at the End of the Tunnel

PASSPORT AND OTHER VISAS

If you haven't got a valid passport already, start to get one at least two months before you plan to go to China. It may take a couple of weeks after submitting the proper photos and documents to receive your passport, and then the Chinese may want to hold your passport a month before you get your China visa.

Some older U.S. passports have a restriction in them against travel to China. If this is the case, better get a new one.

Do not make the mistake of having a visa to the Republic of China (Taiwan) in your passport when you present it to the People's Republic of China (PRC). One Chinese-American who did was given his passport back with a scolding about the "visa by the Chiang Kai-shek gang. This is the way to create two Chinas. Please remove this condition and then send the passport back so that we can execute the visa for you."

He was lucky. He got his visa stamped in another passport. An American newsman, with a long-sought PRC visa in his passport, stopped over in Taiwan on his way to Hong Kong. The PRC refused to let him in.

Make sure also that you have visas if required for all the countries you will be passing through, and remember your own country. I have "permanent resident" status in the United States and discovered on my return that I needed a reentry permit because I had visited a Communist country. My residence card was seized when I reentered the United States, and I was placed on "probation" until I could visit the immigration office and make application for waiver of visa. It was a lot of bother that could have been avoided if I had gotten the reentry permit before leaving the United States.

Check also about your employer. Some governments insist that civil servants clear with them before going to China. Your employer may also insist.

Check also about customs duties in your own country. Find out what you can bring or mail back duty-free. Some countries have forbidden the importation of goods from China.

SHOTS

In addition to a valid passport, you will need an international vaccination book (usually yellow) into which is stamped proof that you have had a smallpox vaccination within three years and two cholera shots within six months of visiting China. Your cholera shots may have to be a month apart, so don't leave them until it is too late. Overseas Chinese and those passing through Africa and South America will in addition need a yellow fever shot.

32

These can usually be obtained from a county health department, a private physician, some Red Cross Societies—just be sure that whoever gives you the shot is eligible to stamp your official certificate. Make sure you also have the required shots for all the countries you will be traveling through, and for your return to your own country.

While the above shots are the only ones required for entry to China, some cautious travelers have also gotten protection against typhoid, typhus, tetanus, diphtheria, and hepatitis—not necessarily for China, but for all the areas they would be traveling in.

COSTS

(See also Finances in Chapter 4 and Sample Prices in Chapter 15.) Visiting China is not cheap, unless you are an expense-paid guest of the state, an Overseas Chinese, or some other exception.

In 1974, expenses for a Foreign Friend traveling alone came to about U.S.$50 a day inside China. Accommodations and travel were first class; there was no other choice. There are no youth hostels, and hitchhiking is prohibited. Travelers cannot tour in their own cars around China.

Group tours are cheaper of course. In 1974, one Chinese-American group was advertising a month's trip—U.S.$575 for transportation from Washington, D.C., to Hong Kong plus U.S.$500 for all expenses in China for a month.

Not all Foreign Friends going to China are fabulously wealthy. Candice Bergen mentions that the expenses of the less affluent members of her group were shared by the others.

The 1973 Downsview Secondary School group from Ontario, Canada, raised Can. $35,000 ($10,000 from Xerox) toward their expenses in addition to the $300 paid by each of the twenty-five high school students who participated. Luxingshe charged them a lower daily rate, and the embassy in Ottawa refunded all visa costs when it discovered the students were financing the program on their own initiative.

Overseas Chinese can cut costs by staying with relatives if they have the room. If you're polite, you will take gifts, but these do not have to cost as much as food and bed in a hotel. Even if you do stay at an Overseas Chinese hotel, you can cut costs by sharing a room with three other people. You can eat in noodle shops and buy all kinds of yummy buns and take public transportation wherever you go—even to the Great Wall. "Hard-class" trains, intercity buses, and overnight boats are cheap.

Of course, the cheaper way takes even more physical stamina and time, but since Overseas Chinese are allowed to stay longer than most foreigners, it can and has been done.

Many travelers can help finance their trip by making arrangements to lecture or write articles or show slides for a fee on their return. You could ask any organization you think might be interested if it has funds available to help you in return for your reporting back on subjects of its special interest.

4
Before You Go

LANGUAGE

Peking dialect is understood by many people all over China. But the local speech varies: Cantonese, Fukienese, Shanghai dialect, etc.—none of which is intelligible to the other. If you want to take lessons beforehand, Peking dialect is more practical if you are traveling around the country; but if you are sticking to the south and living in Chinese homes in Canton and Kwangtung province, then learn Cantonese. The same applies to Fukien or Shanghai.

Chinese writing, however, is understood throughout China. Chinese characters used in China today have been simplified since 1949, and Chinese living outside China have a hard time understanding them unless they have kept up with the changes. Just make sure that whoever teaches you Chinese writing teaches the new script and the *pin yin* romanization. While romanization is not commonly used in China, you will see it on stores, railway stations, and street signs, especially in the north. And a lot of people will be able to understand it.

It might also be helpful to learn the Chinese for commonly used phrases like "serve the people," "American imperialism," and "Cultural Revolution," and polite phrases like "how are you?" "good morning," and "thank you." The word for "comrade" (pronounced *tung chi* in Cantonese and *tung jer* in Peking dialect) is very useful, as it can be used to address everybody but relatives. (See Chapter 19 for Useful Phrases.)

Learn the character for Mao (see Chapter 19). It is easy; you'll see it on signs everywhere.

Don't expect too much. Chinese is a very difficult language to learn. It might take two years of full-time study to be conversationally fluent—longer if you are learning those characters.

LEARNING ABOUT CHINA

To get the most out of your trip, learn something about China before you go.

There is a dizzying list of books on China, a few of which (including details of publications I cite below) are mentioned in the Bibliography. If you know nothing about China, a very elementary booklet is John Roderick's *What You Should Know about the People's Republic of China.* Try a historical survey book like the Macmillan Company's *China's Three Thousand Years* or Ray Wylie's *China: An Introduction for Canadians.*

If you want to know what a typical tour is like, read either John Kenneth Galbraith's *A China Passage,* or J. Tuzo Wilson's *Unglazed China,* Emmett Dedmon's *China Journal,* or Candice Bergen's article in *Playboy* magazine. While none of these writers is a serious student of China, each one will give you a good idea of what to expect. Economist Galbraith is witty; Bergen writes humorously about the effect of China on her fellow travelers and herself. Dedmon sees China with a journalist's eye; and Wilson, a prominent geophysicist on his second trip, has a scientist's mind for tedious detail that may be helpful to other scientists.

Another good introduction is *China Day by Day* by Eileen Hsü-Balzer and Francis L. K. Hsu, with over 150 excellent photographs by Richard J. Balzer. The two Chinese-speaking anthropologists discuss the differences in travel arrangements for Overseas Chinese and foreigners, and describe the differences between America and old China in attitudes about sexuality, human relationships, and religion. Unfortunately, the book does not satisfactorily point out these differences between old and new China. It gives the usual statistics and descriptions of communes, schools, and factories.

If you want to go deeper, try Harrison E. Salisbury's *To Peking—and Beyond* and Ross Terrill's *800,000,000: The Real China*. Both of these writers are long-time students of China, and it shows. Salisbury will make you glad you aren't also going to North Korea.

If you're hooked by now and want something more meaty, then read Edgar Snow, Felix Greene, and Jan Myrdal, who, being friends of the government, have been allowed to see more than the average visitor. Then there are the China scholars like Doak Barnett and John K. Fairbank, and the many books of C. P. Fitzgerald. They are good, but they are outsiders looking in.

More personal accounts are: refugee Ken Ling's *The Revenge of Heaven,* written almost like a sex-and-violence novel, as he relates his life as a student leader during the Cultural Revolution; Bao Ruo-wang/Jean Pasqualini's *Prisoner of Mao,* about a Chinese-Frenchman's seven years in a Chinese prison; Jack Chen's *A Year in Upper Felicity,* about a Peking-based government official's experiences on a commune during the Cultural Revolution; and William G. Sewell's *I Stayed in China,* about a sympathetic British teacher's involvement in the changes at a west China university at the time of Liberation.

The first two books are somewhat hostile, but I include them to give you some balance.

I haven't found a good book yet about Overseas Chinese visiting China, but *Going Back,* though I think it's badly edited, is revealing as it gives the impressions of a group of young Chinese-Americans during a 1972 visit to relatives in Kwangtung province.

Jan C. Ting's *An American in China* starts getting interesting once he stops telling about his group tour (which is much like everyone else's) and writes about his experiences as an Overseas Chinese.

"Fei Ling's Diary in China," serialized by *Bridge,* the Asian-American magazine, is excellent, though I don't agree with many of her conclusions; and of course there is my own article from the *National Observer,* " 'New' China Has an Old Face," a blow-by-blow description of two days in my grandfather's village in Toy Shan in 1973.

If you want a short survey on archaeological work done in China since 1949, do read articles by Dr. Anneliese Gutkind Bulling in *Expedition.*

The best Western news sources are *The New York Times,* the Toronto *Globe and Mail,* and the *Far Eastern Economic Review.* For travel information, *Nagel's Encyclopedia-Guide China* can't be beat. It discusses Chinese history, geography, language, religion, philosophy, art, architecture, economy, and cooking, as well as travel information and maps of places like the Ming tombs, many cities, Tiger Hill in Soochow, and many gardens in Soochow—it is that thorough!

Fodor's *Peking* by Odile Cail is great for Peking if you are going to spend more than a week in the capital, and especially if you are wandering around on your own. She describes the best shopping places, walking tours, off-the-beaten-track temples, and top restaurants—as well as the usual tourist attractions.

S. C. Tao's *The Guide to China* is helpful, but the places it details are limited to Canton, Changsha, Wuhan, Peking, Shenyang, Anshan, Fushun, Tientsin, Tsinan, Nanking, Wusih, Soochow, Shanghai, and Hangchow.

The material published by the Chinese government is as one-sided as publications from any government; but it should be read to give you an idea of the kind of information you will be getting in briefings in China. Do read the famous "little red book," *Quotations from Chairman Mao Tsetung,* so you'll recognize the source of many of the ideas you'll hear expressed in China.

Magazines like *China Reconstructs* and *China Pictorial* are easy reading and have articles about many of the places you will be visiting, descriptions of Chinese movies, the current folk heroes, the current campaigns, and economic achievements. The *Peking Review* is heavy—speeches and policy statements—if you're interested in that kind of thing.

Easy reading also is *The People's Comic Book,* translations of comic books, some of which are still popular in China. These give good insights into the values China wants to instill in her young.

Some groups organize orientation sessions or seminars before they go. The Downsview students took part in six weeks of intensive study twice weekly after the normal school day. Their subjects included the geography, culture, history, and government of China.

Resources included the Chinese embassy, which provided films, and universities, the Royal Ontario Museum, and the Canadian Government.

In the United States, the National Committee on U.S.-China Relations (see Chapter 16) can help. It was set up in 1966 as "a nonpartisan educational organization to encourage public interest in, and understanding of, China and its relations with the United States."

It can help you set up your orientation sessions, suggest program materials, speakers, and other resources. A subscription ($2 a year as we go to press) to its quarterly newsletter will bring you news about visitors to China and Chinese groups to the United States.

The *Understanding China Newsletter* contains interpretative articles, but is not a scholarly journal; at press time it is $3 a year. Recent articles have been on revolutionary literature, a comparison of peasant life in the People's Republic with that on Taiwan, and the Lin Piao and Confucius campaigns.

Learning About Your Own Country:

This is indispensable in your preparation for China. Visit a factory in your own country and learn so you can compare such things as incentives to work, unions, employee benefits, maternity leave, child care for working mothers, job security, and so forth.

When was the last time you were in a school? Find out what subjects are taught at what level, how discipline is maintained, how many to a class, "open" classrooms, "new math," teacher qualifications, incentives to learning, the real cost of education and what happens when a child cannot afford it, report cards, the slow learners, the exceptionally bright child, and the handicapped. How is education financed and who makes the decisions as to what children should learn? Take your notes with you to China so you can ask how the Chinese deal with these things. And with good facts on hand, you can help to clear up Chinese misconceptions about your country.

WRITING TO INDIVIDUALS IN CHINA

It is good practice to write ahead of time to people you especially want to see. Do ask for their telephone numbers, so you can call when you arrive. Officials and scholars could arrange their schedules to meet yours if they knew in advance when you were coming.

Chinese friends and relatives will have time to arrange for leave (with pay) from their jobs to visit with you, or to let you know that you'd better not look them up. If you receive no reply, it could mean they are not interested, or you have the wrong address, or they are terrible letter writers. Sorry I can't decide for you.

As I mentioned before, China goes through xenophobic periods. It also goes through periods of intensive political campaigns where individuals are so busy with meetings, demonstrations, and making "Big Character Posters," they can't take time off.

If China is going through such a period, your friends probably have to explain at great length to fellow workers and cadres how they know you, who you are, what communications you have had with them—a great

41

deal of bother. If they are "capitalist" class or suspected of deviating in any way from party ideals, contact with you may be the straw that sets off an intensive criticism session for them that may result in a remolding trip to a commune.

You will have to weigh all this with how strongly you feel about looking up people you are unsure about. And don't forget your letters will probably be opened and read by officials before your friends receive them.

If you get replies welcoming you to China, then you can make plans to see them. If you have only a couple of days in their city and do not know your exact itinerary ahead of time, you could telegraph them after you arrive in China to contact you at the hotel or through the travel service on your expected arrival date in their city.

Gifts:

Overseas Chinese in particular may want to write to ask what gifts their relatives would like. Don't be surprised if they want a radio, watch, bicycle, or sewing machine. Everyone in Kwangtung seems to know what is allowed in duty-free. You might be able to arrange for other relatives abroad to help pay for expensive gifts. If you cannot afford it, take a less expensive gift and they will (or should) be happy to see you anyway.

HOW YOU CAN BE REACHED IN CHINA

Mail can be addressed to you c/o the organization responsible for your travel—Luxingshe, the Overseas Chinese Travel Service, the Chinese Academy of Sciences, etc. It could also be addressed to you c/o your hotel or even c/o your country's embassy in Peking (assuming you can go there to pick it up).

If you are touring and do not know your hotels and dates, have your letters addressed to you, for example:

> c/o Luxingshe (Chicago Study Group)
> Peking
> People's Republic of china

The "People's Republic of China" should never be abbreviated or the letters will be returned to the sender.

But beware. I once saw a letter addressed to a foreign visitor c/o Luxingshe, Canton, on the "Lost Telegrams" bulletin board in the Overseas Chinese Mansion in Canton. It was nowhere near Luxingshe. So I do suggest you put the Chinese characters for Luxingshe or Overseas Chinese Travel Service or Tung-fang Hotel or whatever on the envelopes your friends and family will send to you. You could have a Chinese friend do this ahead of time on gummed stickers in Chinese and English, so there will be no mistaking your host organization. Few people in south China can understand our alphabet, it seems.

Overseas Chinese in particular should use both Chinese and English names on correspondence with Chinese officials. If you don't know how to write your name in Chinese, then learn. If you don't have a Chinese name, get one. It doesn't have to be legal, but it will make things easier for you as you travel around China.

I had a hard time collecting my mail at the Overseas Chinese Mansion in Canton since my husband neglected to write my Chinese name, under which I was registered, on the envelope, and hardly anyone read English there.

Incidentally, Overseas Chinese would do well to

take along the names of relatives born in China, the names of ancestral villages, and particularly the names of ancestors born in China. This is so your relatives, who may not know of you otherwise, will know just who you are in relation to someone they do know. These names of course should be in Chinese.

Air mail from the United States and Canada takes about ten days; mail to America from China takes about four. Maybe this has something to do with the international date line, but I think it's the time needed for the censors to read incoming mail.

You can also be reached by cable.

There is also international telephone service with the major cities, although there may be problems with language; but do have your home base try if they need to contact you that way. If you cannot be reached c/o Luxingshe (pronounced Liu-shing sher) or your hotel, your home base could phone your country's embassy in Peking and ask them to find you and tell you to telephone home.

It is also possible to send articles by parcel post. There is, however, a very heavy duty placed on goods going into China.

FINANCES

(See also the section on Costs in Chapter 3.) In 1974, travelers with Luxingshe were given a quotation for their total expenses in China and asked to remit this amount *fifteen days prior* to their arrival in China. This was done through any branch or correspondent of the Bank of China into Luxingshe's account. The rate of exchange was that of the day of payment.

44

On the last day in China, accounts were tallied and additional payments or refunds were made. It will probably be the same now, but Luxingshe will tell you what the current procedure is.

Businessmen and Overseas Chinese pay as they go.

U.S., Canadian, and Hong Kong dollars, British pounds and Japanese yen, traveler's checks and cash were converted into Chinese currency at the border when I was there. There will probably be no trouble with other currencies, but do ask before you go.

There is no limit to the amount of money you can carry into China just as long as it isn't China's own currency. When you change money in China, you will be given a receipt that customs officials will ask for on your way out, as well as the certificate noting the foreign currency you have brought in. Each time you change money, a note of the amount will be made on this certificate.

It is illegal to give foreign currency to anyone else in China; it is also illegal to take out Chinese currency. Some people carry letters of credit obtained from a Chinese bank before entering China, but these do not seem as convenient to cash as traveler's checks. Convert only what you need for a few days at a time as it is difficult to reconvert large amounts at the border on the way out. If you must reconvert, it would be better to go to the Bank of China in the last city you are in. It is a time-consuming procedure, forty-five minutes by one estimate.

You can also obtain an envelope at the border to send back unspent Chinese currency to friends or relatives in China.

Most hotels will have Service Desks where you can change your money. You can also change it at Friendship Stores and, of course, at any bank.

Take enough money with you; you will not be able to pay in stores with personal checks, although some American businessmen at the 1974 spring trade fair said they paid for goods with personal checks. You could try to get your embassy to cash a personal check, but don't count on it. If you need more money, you can have it cabled to you through the Bank of China. Your home bank will need to know your passport number. Remittances must be picked up at the Bank of China's main offices. Give yourself five banking days for money cabled to you.

Your home bank may not be able to deal directly with the Bank of China, but it undoubtedly has a corresponding relationship with some bank that does know how to make a transaction. Most Canadian banks (or their branches in New York City and San Francisco), the Chartered Bank, the Hongkong and Shanghai Banking Corporation, Chase Manhattan, Banque Nationale de Paris, and a few others can help you directly.

Comparison Shopping:

If you are a serious shopper intent on bargains, I suggest doing some homework and keeping notes. You're going to have to do some comparison shopping before you go. I'd tell you the best buys, except that prices keep changing.

First of all, many goods you can buy in China are available abroad, and one traveler related sadly how the painted eggs she bought in China were the same price she found later in a Washington store. So look around at home, especially in local Chinatowns where prices are usually cheaper than in downtown Chinese-American curio stores, and make notes on prices.

On the whole, however, the choice for bargains is really between Hong Kong (see Chapter 5) and China (see Chapter 11). If you are going to enter and leave China through Hong Kong, try to spend several days each time you pass through.

The Chinese government has stores in Hong Kong selling nothing but goods made in the mainland, sometimes at prices cheaper than in China! I suggest you price the items you want there, check the prices for the same things in China, and take the cheaper.

Calculate also the fact that Americans and Canadians have only a $100 duty-free allowance on goods purchased abroad. Anything over that allowance is subject to duties (and in Canada, to excise taxes and federal sales taxes as well) that could be as high as an additional 50 percent. Also add the cost of shipping or excess baggage.

U.S. Customs:

They have a booklet, *Know Before You Go,* which lists duty rates, but not on goods from Communist countries, which are higher. The booklet is helpful, so do get it; but also phone the customs office closest to you about rates on things like rugs, which you might be interested in.

Canadian Customs:

They also have a leaflet, but it does not spell out rates. I have listed some of these rates in Chapter 11.

WHAT TO TAKE

Items for personal use are allowed into China duty-free. Overseas Chinese can take in a list of duty-exempt items as gifts. (See section on Overseas Chinese in Chapter 2.) Duty is sometimes as high as 80 percent to bring the cost of an item up to Chinese prices. A fellow traveler of mine was charged ¥18 (U.S.$9) on a blanket he was bringing in. Another was given the choice of paying duty or leaving one of his two cameras behind at the border to be picked up on his way out.

Both these travelers were Overseas Chinese, who are very carefully searched at the border. But there is a degree of flexibility. After searching through my luggage for twenty minutes, the four customs officials assigned to me had a meeting, and decided to let me take in, duty-free, items that are normally dutiable.

Another Overseas Chinese wept when told she couldn't take her typewriter in. (I had no trouble about mine.) Customs officials relented.

China visitors sometimes may have to carry their own luggage, so keep this in mind as you pack.

Clothing:

From November to March, north China is bitterly cold and many of the buildings are not heated. No, don't worry about your hotel, you'll be warm there. The Chinese sometimes lend visitors heavy padded coats for trips to the coldest, windiest spot of all—the Great Wall—but even then, you should take along your own long, thermal underwear.

I suggest you do as the natives do; plan on layers of clothing and a loose-fitting top coat rather than one thick heavy coat that will be excess baggage in the springlike south. Peking has snow and freezing weather, so warm boots are also essential.

The rainy season in the south is March to May, with rain or drizzle almost every day. It starts getting hot in April. The Chinese wear plastic or cloth sandals because mold grows on leather. An umbrella or light plastic raincoat is helpful.

All of China is hot in the summer, especially Chungking, Nanking, and Wuhan, which are known as the "three furnaces." And you can probably count the number of air conditioned buildings on one hand. Let me know if you find anything comfortably cool besides the Friendship Stores and the International Club.

If you don't mind being stared at, wear what you want as long as it is comfortable and not too extreme. I saw a couple of miniskirts but no hot pants on visiting women. I suggest no halters. You may be mistaken for a prostitute if you wear too little. Pants suits are right in style since Chinese women wear trousers and, for you, the wide trousers will be great for climbing into buses. The steps are high.

Shorts for men are ideal in the summer. The natives are going to stare at you anyway, even if you are Overseas Chinese, but you can minimize the attention with conservative clothing, especially dark blues and grays. Some Overseas Chinese visitors bought Mao jackets in Hong Kong and blended with the scenery. But a Foreign Friend in a Mao jacket still attracts attention. Mao jackets are known in China as cadre jackets.

It is sometimes advantageous to appear different from the local population, however. Special courtesies are extended to visitors; sometimes you may not have to wait so long in lines for bicycle rickshaws for example, and frequently people on buses will give up their seats for you.

At the same time, looking different tends to isolate you from people and make you an object of curiosity. Such is the dilemma.

Laundry and dry cleaning service at hotels is done in one day, so don't worry about drip-dry clothing if you're going to be in Canton during the rainy season. Pure cotton or predominantly cotton mixtures are better for the heat there. I tried washing my own things, but the humidity kept them from getting dry in less than two days.

If you will be moving around from city to city, staying one or two days in each, better take several changes of clothing. You may not have a chance to get them laundered.

Dress for comfort. Do take good walking shoes, because you will be on your feet a lot and climbing stairs. Once, in 1965, after a day of sight-seeing, I arrived at a formal banquet, hosted by Premier Chou En-lai, in the slacks and sweater I had been wearing all day. No one seemed to mind or notice.

Chinese men do not wear ties and on hot days sometimes show up at formal banquets with just trousers and a white shirt open at the collar. You might feel more secure dressing up a bit more than that for formal occasions, but high heels and evening gowns for women are impractical, unless you expect a formal reception hosted by foreign diplomats. Lots of jewelry and makeup will make you look decadently bourgeois in Chinese company.

Most tour schedules are booked solid, but you may be able to squeeze in a swim after May. So take a bathing suit if you want.

Don't count on buying everyday clothes in China. You need to have coupons for cotton goods; and the selection in the Friendship Store, where you don't need coupons, is generally limited to luxury-quality things like hand-embroidered blouses and cashmere sweaters.

Toiletries:

On communes, and even in the restroom at the border, there is no toilet paper. Overseas Chinese may even find it lacking in their hotels, and certainly missing in their relatives' homes. It is wise to carry a few tissues with you just in case.

If you are fussy, take your favorite brands of shampoo, toothpaste, shaving cream, soap, sanitary napkins, and other toiletries. China has its own equivalents, which you can buy in your hotel's retail store, but I found the toothpaste very sweet and perfumed (someone else has found ginseng-flavored toothpaste), and most things are more expensive than in Hong Kong. You will find very few foreign goods in China, and who wants to spend time looking? Chinese women do not wear cosmetics, so you won't find much of these either.

Shortwave Transistor Radio:

To get world news. You may otherwise get nothing. The Voice of America news is broadcast on the 13, 16, 19, 25, 31, and 49 meter bands. The British Broadcasting Corporation can be heard in north and east China on the 31, 41, 49, and 75 meter bands, and in south China on the 13, 16, 25, 31, and 41 meter bands.

It is possible to rent a radio in some but not all

hotels, and there are no English-language newspapers for sale.

Camera and Film:

Customs officers may let you take in more than twenty rolls of film, but this is what they told me was the official limit. Film is available in China but it may not be in your size. Chinese customs reserves the right to have all exposed film processed before being taken out of the country. However, at this time, the Chinese are not enforcing this regulation strictly. It is, however, a chance you are taking if you use film like Kodachrome, which cannot be processed there.

China does process Ektachrome, Kodacolor, Agfacolor, Sakuracolor, and black and white. But the quality of the processing is not always good. I have usually had good luck in Canton, but terrible processing in Peking.

China does not make color prints, nor does it mount slides. Your slide film will be returned instead in a long roll that you can have cut up and mounted into slides when you get to Hong Kong (cheaper) or home. In 1973, it cost U.S.$3 to process a roll of Ektachrome in China, and then U.S. two cents a slide to have them mounted in Hong Kong.

Be sure to take in extra flash batteries and flash cubes, as these are not available in China.

Maps and Books:

If you're carrying a map of China, be careful that Taiwan is shown as part of the People's Republic or you may be embarrassed by a scolding.

You can usually buy good maps in English of the main cities at the hotel or a department store.

A Chinese-English dictionary is superfluous if you have a bilingual person with you most of the time, but a dictionary and a phrase book will be useful if you aren't completely fluent with the language and you're wandering around on your own. Don't take a heavy, detailed guidebook unless you want more than the basic facts on the tourist sites that your human guide will provide. Take one, though, if you want to compare your guide's facts with your guidebook.

If you will be discussing very technical terms, you may want these translated before you go so there will be no question of being misunderstood. Interpreters will not know how to translate terms the average English-speaking person doesn't even understand in English.

Nagel's guide (see Learning About China above and the Bibliography) is over 1500 pages, and weighs almost two pounds. If you are going in a group and want to have it, maybe you can share one. Your guide will give you a very superficial description of any place you will see, so take it if you want a little more detail or if you will be without a guide.

It is forbidden to import books "detrimental to the politics, economy, culture, and ethics of the People's Republic of China."

Medicines and Vitamins:

Take in what you need for your visit since exact Chinese equivalents may be hard to find. The Chinese do have antibiotics. Take in salt tablets and talcum powder for hot weather if you need them, and cold tablets for colds. You can buy liquid mosquito repellent and anti-

53

mosquito incense coils in China—yes, there are mosquitoes in Canton during the rainy season.

Gifts:

Unless you are a head-of-state, the gifts you take to China should be inexpensive—more of the souvenir type. The Chinese are very sensitive about anything that smacks of bribery and corruption. Tipping is forbidden because it is insulting; people serve you because they want to help, not because they want your money. The same goes for any gifts, and even your "Responsible Person" will usually decline gifts meant for him personally.

One visitor got around this by presenting a large Webster's dictionary to the Luxingshe *office.*

It is not necessary to give gifts, but if you must, Canadian delegations have given out maple leaf pins; Americans might do the same with pins of the American flag or your city's name and emblem.

Postcards or colorful tourist pictures of your home town are accepted with interest. Tuzo Wilson distributed pictures of Norman Bethune's birthplace in Canada, Bethune being almost a Chinese saint. You'll see Bethune's statue in many places in China.

Frisbees and Slinkies, crayons, and colored marking pencils are great for children. Individual children loved animal picture storybooks, but I would hesitate to give any books to schools and kindergartens. They could be considered subversive. The values promoted in our children's literature are different from the realistic Chinese children's books that glorify workers, peasants, soldiers, hard work, selflessness, and thrift.

Delegations might give some distinctive souvenir related to their special interests—labeled North American rock specimens, a periodic chart, medical books, etc., and authors might want to give copies of their books (if appropriate).

One great way to be popular—but quickly broke—is to take and pass out Polaroid photos of the people you meet, especially in color. If you are invited to a home, especially for a meal, it is customary to take fruit or candy or, again, a souvenir from your home—but nothing elaborate. You might take something for your host's children.

Miscellaneous:

If you're fussy about your coffee and tea, take in some instant coffee or your own tea bags, powdered cream, sugar, and a spoon. Chinese coffee tastes different. Chinese hotels provide cups and a big thermos of hot water every day (actually meant for Chinese tea).

I found a jackknife handy for cutting fruit for snacks, and a flashlight for dark houses and for late-night walks as a precaution against lightless bicycles and trucks.

If you're fussy about your liquor, especially Scotch or bourbon, take some in with you—you're allowed to take in a reasonable supply for your own use. You can buy Chinese liquors and beer in your hotel. Chinese brandy and vodka have been described as "outstanding."

Note that Chinese appliances are 220V (U.S. and Canada use 110V) and use three-pronged plugs. Some hotels have adapters and transformers, but not all. You may have to take your own adapter if you have an electric razor.

Also note that drugs such as opium and morphine are forbidden.

And don't forget a notebook!

5
Getting There

BY REGULARLY SCHEDULED AIRLINES

The following airlines have direct service to China or soon will have: Air France, Aeroflot, British Airways, Civil Aviation Administration of China, Civil Aviation Administration DPR Korea, Canadian Pacific Airlines, Ethiopian Airlines, Finnair, Japan Air Lines, Pakistan International Airlines, and Royal Air Lao.

Chinese cities served by these international flights are: Nanning, Peking, Kunming, Shenyang, Shanghai, and Canton—but you will probably be allowed to disembark only in Peking, Shanghai, or Canton if you're coming from abroad.

BY CHEAPER WAYS

If you're starting from the eastern part of North America, try to avoid paying regular IATA fares; look into cheaper flights to Europe offered by non-IATA members such as Icelandic, advance-payment plans offered by supplemental carriers such as Laker and Wardair in Canada or World in the United States, or special bargain fares offered by organizations, travel agents, and often by IATA carriers themselves.

Look into the Air France 7–45-day excursion to Peking or the Pakistan International Airlines 14–21-day excursion to Peking via Karachi. Or take PIA's 15–120-day excursion from New York City to Karachi and then their 14–21-day excursion from Karachi to Peking, which will give you more time in China. Depending on the rate of exchange, this method might save you money, since you pay for the second leg with rupees in Karachi (but count on a couple of days in Karachi).

Do plan carefully or your bargain may turn out to be more expensive. For example, some supplemental carrier fares are only for forty-five days and only across the Atlantic. Unless you hook up with another bargain flight, it might turn out to be more expensive.

You will need a computer to save money, and a budget for phone calls to airline offices, unless you have a willing travel agent.

VIA HONG KONG

Hong Kong is an ideal place to have a rest after a long transoceanic flight. "Jet lag," the time it takes your body to adjust to a different clock, sometimes takes a week to overcome.

Hong Kong is serviced by many ships and airlines as well as by many charter associations offering cheaper fares. If you are going there from Britain, the United States, Canada, or some parts of Southeast Asia, there are many special charters flying regularly for persons of Chinese origin, and some charters for anyone regardless of origin.

Charters:

These usually have every seat booked so you cannot stretch out to sleep. They frequently don't leave on time because regularly scheduled airlines have a higher priority at international airports. You are limited also because you must return with the same company within a certain time limit on their flight schedule, which may be twice a month.

But if these problems don't bother you, you will save several hundred dollars from North America or Europe to Hong Kong.

Some charter organizations require some sort of membership fee (sometimes only a nominal fee of a dollar or so) and enrollment as much as six months before you fly. Some ignore this time limit, and also allow non-Chinese spouses on Overseas Chinese charters.

Excursion Flights:

Airlines going to India offer a very low (21-120-day) excursion fare from New York City to New Delhi, Bombay, or Calcutta. By buying an additional ticket from New Delhi to Hong Kong and spending at least one night in India both ways, you will be paying less than regular fare from the eastern part of North America. Your travel agent can do this without the New York-

India carrier knowing about it—IATA regulations and all that. Excursion passengers cannot make stopovers, but do fly on regularly scheduled airlines, so there is a chance of stretching out to sleep on empty seats.

Korean Airlines has a cheap 21-day excursion to Hong Kong from California, I hear. Air Siam is another non-IATA airline that has special rates. Shop around. You may save a lot of money.

IF YOU'RE YOUNG OR
YOUNG AT HEART

The possibilities of getting to China relatively cheaply are wide open. But you need lots of time.

There are buses from London to New Delhi for a little over U.S.$100 and regular direct bus service from Munich to Teheran, with local land transport from there to India. Ask about these around YMCA's or Youth Hostels or wherever traveling young people hang out. The Munich bus used to leave near the Munich railway station.

You might try going by motorcycle or jeep. I do not recommend hitchhiking; I think it's dangerous, especially in West Asia.

Anyway, if the bus will drop you off in Pakistan, you could take a plane from Karachi to Peking; otherwise you could take a third-class train (book ten days in advance) to Calcutta from New Delhi, and then a ship to Hong Kong. Sorry, I don't recommend the overland route through Southeast Asia as long as there are travel restrictions in Burma, and fighting in Cambodia and Vietnam.

The overland route might prove to be more expensive than the New York-New Delhi excursion flight, but it'll be a lot more interesting.

Another way, cheaper than flying, is by train from Paris to Moscow and then the Trans-Siberian railroad to Peking. (Six days Moscow-Peking.) There are also trains from Hanoi, Pyongyang, Ulan Bator, and Hong Kong. Some people enter via the Portuguese colony of Macao. Most travelers enter via Hong Kong.

A list of some of the charter companies is in Chapter 16.

HONG KONG

While its prices have risen over the years, Hong Kong is still one of the best bargain cities of the world, with its duty-free prices for cameras, watches, and radios, and its relatively cheap sandals and clothes, but not for books, which are about the same price as in North America. Stock up on supplies you need for China. In 1973, Kodachrome film cost half the U.S. price.

The Chinese government emporiums in Hong Kong, such as Yue Hwa, will have up-to-date lists of what Overseas Chinese can take in duty-free, and will even pack and ship these to the railway station if you give them more than one day's notice.

Some people have found that some items in these government emporiums, especially the one at Nathan and Jordan Roads in Kowloon, are cheaper than in China; and there is also more variety in Hong Kong. Don't forget to price the item you want in Hong Kong, then compare it with the price in China, and take the cheaper. For additional tips, see also "Comparison Shopping" in Chapter 4, as well as Chapter 11.

Don't forget that in the smaller owner-clerk stores in Hong Kong you can haggle. Prices will go up automatically because you are a foreigner, so if there's no one else around, try your hand at the fine art of bargaining. The owner will probably be more stubborn if there is another foreign customer within earshot.

Hong Kong, a British colony, was formerly part of China (the Chinese still consider it such), and parts are scheduled to revert back to China in the 1990s. It is extremely crowded because of the refugees from China. You can get some of the flavor of Old China, especially in the isolated villages on Lan Tao Island or the New Territories—the temples, festivals, elaborate funeral customs, dirt, purse snatchers, and extremes of wealth. It is a good introduction for the contrast of new China next door, and it might be good for you to talk with refugees from China—why did they risk their lives to leave? Welfare agencies can help you contact Chinese refugees.

China Travel Service:

This office in Hong Kong (see also page 13) will give you information about train times; there are two leaving early every morning, connecting with Chinese trains at the border. The train leaves from Kowloon Station (to the right as you leave the Star Ferry). There are no flights from Hong Kong to China, but a helicopter service to Canton has been proposed and air service to other cities is under discussion.

The China Travel Service will arrange for your tickets and help with your luggage, picking it up at your Hong Kong address and delivering it to the railway station.

BEING MET IN CHINA

It is standard procedure in China to travel under the wing of some agency—Luxingshe, the Overseas Chinese Travel Service, the Academy of Science, or some other host agency. One does not just arrive at an airport and plan to take a taxi to a hotel or a relative's home. There are no taxis at airports unless they have been booked in advance. In addition, only persons with special permission can go to airports.

If you are flying directly into China, make sure that your host agency knows when you are arriving. Overseas Chinese can arrange to meet relatives at an Overseas Chinese hotel. You don't have to worry about being met if you go through Hong Kong. The China Travel Service there alerts the relevant organizations automatically, and relatives are allowed to meet your train.

If by some mistake or natural calamity you are not met and language is a problem, point to the characters for Luxingshe or whatever in Chapter 19, and hope that someone will contact your hosts.

Reporting to the Police:

If you arrive by air, besides having your passport stamped by immigration officials and your luggage cleared by customs, *you should report to the police* or Public Security Office, who have a desk with a sign in English to that effect, at the airport. Your Responsible Person should do this for you, while you rest and drink tea.

Customs:

The same customs regulations apply here as at the Hong Kong border, although I know one Overseas Chinese who was charged duty in Shanghai on a watch she was bringing in to a friend. I don't guarantee any exemptions. Maybe, if customs tries to make you pay, you could argue that you heard Overseas Chinese were allowed one watch in addition to their own. In any case, you can leave it at customs to be picked up on the way out.

IF YOU TAKE THE TRAIN FROM HONG KONG TO CANTON

The train from Kowloon to Lo Wu, the Hong Kong border point, takes about one hour. As a Foreign Friend or Overseas Chinese, you will be afforded special treatment. A representative of the China Travel Service will be at the station to assist you and you may check all your luggage to the border at no extra cost. You will be riding first class.

Standard tip for a railway station porter in 1973 was one Hong Kong dollar (U.S. twenty cents) per bag from the curb to the China Travel Service meeting point.

At Lo Wu (the stop after Sheung Shui), you will have your passport stamped by Hong Kong authorities and then you will walk across the bridge into China, to the town of Shumchun. Photos are permitted. You can ask your friendly Travel Service man to take one of you on the bridge.

You will be taken to comfortable waiting rooms and

served tea while your passport and health certificates are checked and you fill out a customs declaration form. You may have to wait about forty-five minutes. You will then be taken to the customs shed, where you will find all your luggage and baggage. Most Foreign Friends will be waved through, but Overseas Chinese will have their bags opened and minutely inspected. If you need one and are lucky, you may even have an English-speaking customs official checking you. See section on What to Take, Chapter 4.

If your trip is not prepaid, you will be charged for luggage checked from the border at Shumchun to Canton. There is a place to change money after customs clearance, and to pay for the checked luggage—which, for Overseas Chinese, will not appear again for another day. Overseas Chinese should separate what they need for the night and this hand baggage can also be checked. The hand luggage will show up again in the hotel lobby when you do.

There will be time to eat at the border before the train leaves. If you took the 7:30 A.M. train from Kowloon, you will be on the 1:00 P.M. train from Shumchun to Canton, arriving at 2:50 P.M. You may take photos from the train and you will be entertained by music, news, quotations from Chairman Mao, and a speech of welcome in Chinese over the loudspeakers on the train.

By this time you should have adjusted your watch. Hong Kong summer time is one hour ahead of Chinese time.

6
Hotels

The traveler who is cared for by any organization aside from the Overseas Chinese Travel Service doesn't have to worry about logistical details; your Responsible Person will take care of red tape and tickets. But you may have to explain your interests and the visits you would like to make each time you arrive in a new city. If you are in a group, you will probably choose a group leader who will consult with your Responsible Person about daily schedules. Your Responsible Person may also interpret for you, especially if your group is small.

Your Responsible Person will try very hard to meet any special requests you may have, but don't expect all of these to be met. Feel lucky if even one or two can be arranged.

Generally speaking, you have no choice of hotel; feel lucky you have a room. One night my daughter and I had to share one bed in a room with three other women.

If you do want major adjustments, such as changing your room, consult your group leader or Responsible

Person. The service comrade at the desk nearest your hotel room (in other countries known as a room boy) can take care of things such as laundry, soap and towels, adapters for electric razors, and renting radios, electric fans, or portable electric heaters. He can get your photographs developed, and in some hotels will be able to store excess luggage to be picked up later. In many of the ritzier hotels, he can sell you cigarettes or liquor, and provide beer or tea for your guests.

Each hotel has its own policy about locking hotel room doors. Some rooms will be opened for you by your service comrade and the keys kept at his desk; in some places, your key sits on a board at the service desk, and the service comrade may or may not always be present; in other hotels, the room doors are not locked. I have never heard of anything being stolen from a hotel in China; but for your own peace of mind, if you have any valuables, lock them in your suitcase, or ask your Responsible Person if the hotel has a safe.

FACILITIES

Visitors generally agree that most Chinese hotels have excellent food and service. Usually you'll also find elevators. In addition, you'll probably find:

Telephones:

These may be in each room or at the Service Desk. You can call any point in most cities by dialing "*O*" and then your number once you get the dial tone. If it is not a dial phone, tell the operator what number you want.

The Chinese do not have private phones but there

are telephones in every neighborhood, factory, and office, where messages can be left with much assurance that they will be delivered to your friends. I suggest you leave a message to have your friend phone you. In a pinch, the operator might be able to find you a phone number if you give her an address. Needless to say, you'd better get some Chinese-speaking person to help you if you can't handle the language.

You can phone abroad from the main cities, even from your hotel. You have to book the call at the Service Desk, but you can take it in your room when the operator makes the connection. If the service comrade seems reluctant to help or says, "You'll have to wait," it might be because of his lack of English. Offer to speak to the Overseas Operator yourself. That operator should speak English.

Sometimes an overseas call has taken me ten minutes, sometimes an hour to complete. The reception in China was excellent, but there was an interfering echo on the other end of the line. Nevertheless, the messages got through.

The policy of paying for an overseas call differs from city to city. At the Overseas Chinese Mansion in Canton, I had to pay right after the call; in Peking, I could call collect, or have the call put on my hotel bill. There is a service charge even if the call is not completed.

Don't forget the time difference. New York City is thirteen hours behind China, give or take an hour depending on Standard and Daylight time. Thus, 8:00 P.M. China time is 7:00 A.M. New York or Toronto Standard time, 12:00 noon Greenwich Mean Time or 4:00 A.M. San Francisco time.

Post and Telegraph Service:

For outgoing communications, there is usually an office on the ground or second floor of your hotel. Generally these are closed on Sunday morning. Be sure you use the glue pot on your stamps; they are not the licking variety because the humidity in the south would make such stamps stick together. Be sure to glue your envelopes shut.

In some hotels, incoming mail will be delivered to your room; in other hotels you may find it in a pile at the registration desk or with your Responsible Person—or all of these.

A Retail Store:

For such items as soap, toothpaste, fresh fruit, stationery, maps, books, toilet paper, preserved fruit, postcards, and cigarettes, every hotel I've stayed in has had a shop.

Money-Changing Facilities:

Some hotels have a branch of the Bank of China right in the lobby (closed on Sunday). Otherwise the lobby Service Desk will accept your traveler's checks, and several hours later, after a trip to the bank, will have your Chinese currency ready for you.

1 *yuan* = 10 *jiao* or *mao* = 100 *fen*.

Food:

Restaurants are usually on the first two floors; sometimes on the top. Most hotels for Foreign Friends will give you a choice of Chinese or Western food. Of the seven Overseas Chinese hotels I've stayed in, only the Shanghai Overseas Chinese hotel had Western food. Restaurant hours are usually posted outside the restaurant doors. Some restaurants have liquor and snack bar facilities—ice cream, pastries, coffee, soft drinks, etc.

Paying procedures differ. Some hotels have you sign your check; some make you pay your bill as you go out. (See also Chapter 8.)

Travel Service:

The Service Desk in most hotel lobbies, or your Responsible Person, usually takes care of reporting your newly arrived presence to the Public Security office in each city. The Service Desk will also arrange plane and train tickets for you if you need them, taxis, charter buses, and airport transportation. There may be a nearby stand for bicycle rickshaws (also known as pedicabs—and cheap) or scooter rickshaws (also known as three-wheeled taxis—less cheap).

The Service Desk also sells tickets to local cultural events and tours to local factories, communes, and schools. Try them if you need a baby-sitter. They might be able to provide one.

At the Overseas Chinese Mansion in Canton, a separate travel bureau is in the building out the door and to the right. Go in to the left of the huge painting of the Tien An Men and you will also find the retail store there. This travel bureau will also book passage on inter-city boats.

Health Facilities:

Some hotels, for example the Overseas Chinese hotels in Peking and Canton, have their own clinics and doctors. I think this is because many Overseas Chinese stay at these hotels while they are getting medical treatment. Other hotels will refer you to a nearby hospital if you are ill.

Hot Water from a Faucet:

But only during the evenings. And sometimes the showers don't work. Luxury hotels have hot water all day.

Hot Drinking Water:

Every morning in a large thermos left by your door. Cool it in the teapot provided in your room by placing it in a sink of cool water.

Television:

Ask for it if you don't see it in a lobby. Most stations usually broadcast a few hours a day, but don't expect to find Archie Bunker or Walter Cronkite.

Daily Newspapers:

The *Renmin Ribao,* the People's Daily, is usually delivered to Chinese-speaking guests.

Hairdressers and Barbers:

You will find Chinese men wear their hair short and

71

Chinese women have theirs naturally straight and short, or braided. You may not feel the need to spend time fixing your hair. The hotel hairdressing equipment looks ancient, but the massage that comes with a shampoo will have your scalp tingling for days. In some cities, you can get your hair styled the way you want it.

Few, if Any, "Bell Boy" Comrades:

In some hotels, especially the Overseas Chinese ones, there may not be anyone around who is assigned specifically to help carry luggage. This is especially hard on Overseas Chinese in Canton who are importing bicycles and sewing machines and must retrieve these from the building out the door and to the right of the Overseas Chinese Mansion. But there are trolleys you can borrow from the ground floor of the Mansion. There are also trolleys beside the elevators on each floor. You might also ask about having your gifts shipped directly to friends.

Businessmen staying at the Tung-fang Hotel in Canton will have all their luggage delivered to their hotel room.

SPECIAL FEATURES OF SOME HOTELS

(With comments by several visitors; let me know if there have been changes.)

Canton:

Tung-fang Hotel (East Is Red Hotel) is across the street from the Trade Fair building and within a five-minute walk of Yueh-hsiu Park and the new railway station. It is primarily for businessmen attending the Canton Trade Fair, though other groups stay there. Japanese businessmen still use the Kwangchow Hotel, and the Overseas Chinese businessmen use the Overseas Chinese Mansion.

The Tung-fang's attractions include a Telex service, a Canton Fair liaison office to assist businessmen, a billiard room, a huge bar named the "Purple Cockatoo" (open 9:00 P.M. to midnight), and a series of reception chambers. There is also an office of Luxingshe that will take care of police registration formalities. During the trade fairs, there are also offices of the National Council for U.S.-China Trade and the United States Liaison Office. Many foreign governments, including Canada, also have representations there.

East Hotel: Galbraith said it had "cavernous, bright comfortable rooms."

Ren Min Hotel: In the old section of town. Rooms were comfortable, but the plumbing was in disrepair, one guest reported.

Hangchow:

There are three hotels in a row along the lake. The **Gardens of Flowers Hotel** is pleasant in its sylvan setting. Large, comfortable, airy rooms. In 1973, the cooks asked guests what they wanted to eat, and provided gourmet meals for U.S.$1.50 a day.

Nanking:

The **Nanking Hotel** is set in a secluded rose garden. If you're allergic to roses, ask for the **Victory Hotel**.

Peking:

Chien Men (Open Door) is said to be a large hotel with comfortable rooms and television in the lobbies.

Friendship Hotel is in the western suburbs.

Hsin Chiao Hotel is the home of many foreign journalists and visiting cultural delegations. Its sixth-floor restaurant has a good view of the city.

Nationalities Hotel (Min-tzu)—next to the Minorities Palace—is a pleasant walk along a broad boulevard to Tien An Men Square, the Forbidden City, and the Great Hall of the People. One guest told me that it was not as clean as other hotels. Chimes playing "The East Is Red" may awaken you at 7:00 A.M. Room charges were said to include all the tangerines and candy you could eat, and all the beer you could drink. Also included were a haircut, Ping-Pong, and pool tables.

Peking Hotel is usually for high-level delegations. It is at the corner of Wang Fu Ching street, which is the main shopping street, and the boulevard that leads to Tien An Men Square a few minutes walk away. The U.S. Liaison Office was in this hotel until it moved into its own building. An English-language newsheet is delivered to the rooms every day here. A new seventeen-floor, 600-bed wing, opened in 1974, attempts to do away with the grubby, old-world look of most Chinese hotels by the addition of pastel-colored telephones, automatic lobby doors, eight automatically synchronized elevators, and a bar. But there's a glorious view of the Forbidden City from the top floors.

Shanghai:

Chin Chang Hotel: Previously an apartment building, this hotel was the site of the Nixon-Chou Communiqué in 1972. An English-language newsheet is available in the waiting room. Elegant.

International Hotel gets the overflow from the **Overseas Chinese Hotel** next door. Both are on Nanking Road, the main shopping street (to the left as you go out the door) and five minutes walk from the home stage of the Shanghai Acrobats.

Peace Hotel (formerly the Cathay) is great—old-world character, rather posh. Magnificent dining room with spectacular view on top floor. Service comrades speak English. Ping-Pong, pool and haircuts included. Hotel is situated along the waterfront.

Shanghai Mansions: Great view of the Bund from the seventeenth floor, but noisy traffic on the Whangpoo River all night has kept guests awake. Otherwise fine. Near Friendship Store.

Shenyang:

Tourist Hotel, previously the Mukden Railway Hotel, was a center of intrigue during the last days of the civil war in the late 1940s. Pool and billiard tables are from that era.

Sian:

People's Hotel (Ren-min Ta-hsia) is a fifteen-minute walk from the shopping district.

The **Sian Hotel** has 1000 rooms and was originally built for Russian technicians. One group of eight foreign visitors found themselves rattling around as the only guests there.

7

Special to Overseas Chinese

THE OVERSEAS CHINESE TRAVEL SERVICE

If no one has contacted you within two hours of arrival in your hotel, you can ask the service comrade to contact the Overseas Chinese Travel Service. This will save you time, since it takes time to get permission to go anywhere that is not mentioned on your visa. An official will come to your room or ask to meet you in the lobby.

When you get hold of an official, be sure to get his or her name in case you want to contact him later. Permission to travel usually takes two to four days, but it may take up to two weeks. Remember, the Service does not operate at peak efficiency on Sundays or holidays, so make your plans accordingly.

If you are staying with relatives in one of the principal cities, you can still go to the office of the Overseas Chinese Travel Service. It is usually in the Overseas Chinese Hotel.

Plan your itinerary as exactly as you can. I wanted to go from Canton to Sun Wui, back to Canton, and then to Peking and Shanghai by myself. Because I was unsure of the date I would leave Sun Wui, the Travel Service waited until I returned to Canton before applying for permission for the northern trip. Consequently, I had to wait four more days to get that permit, and then four days for a plane ticket. Permission for all my points outside Canton could have been obtained at one time if I had given an exact date for all departures and arrivals, saving me those eight days in Canton.

THINGS TO KEEP HANDY

Valuables such as your passport and your currency declaration form (obtained on entering China). You will need them when you change money.

If you are not on a guided tour, the slip giving you permission to go to other cities is of the greatest importance. You will need it, as well as your passport, to buy travel tickets, get a hotel room, get on a plane, etc. It can be surrendered to the Service Desk when you register at a hotel, but make sure you get it back when you leave. In many cities, you will have it stamped at the airport or train station when you arrive and leave. This policy seems to differ from city to city.

Hang on to the badges given you by the Travel Service and put one on when you travel so that bus drivers, taxi drivers, guides—people meeting you—will know who you are.

OVERSEAS CHINESE HOTELS

The *Overseas Chinese Mansion* (Hwa Chiao Dai Ha) in **Canton** is an old building, grubby and usually very crowded. I saw a rat in my room one night. If the res-

77

taurants are packed, don't hesitate to ask fellow diners if you can use the empty chairs at their table.

The Mansion is conveniently located along the Pearl River and about half a mile from the Nan-fang Dai Ha, the biggest department store, and the Man Fa Goong Yuen, a culture park best seen in the evening.

In 1973, I heard that a new Overseas Chinese hotel was due to open in 1974. Let me know if you stay there.

The *Overseas Chinese Hotel* in **Shanghai** is luxurious by comparison—thick carpets, drapes, stuffed armchairs —a look of affluence from another era at the same prices as Canton. The Overseas Chinese Hotel in **Hangchow** on the lake is very pleasant; and the one in **Peking** on Wang Fu Ching street (there are two) is very clean, bright, cheerful, and utilitarian. No frills except a large, spacious dining room with a high ceiling.

There are *Overseas Chinese hotels* in many small cities that Chinese emigrants left many years ago, and now come back to visit. I have seen them in Kwangtung Province in **Fat Shan** (Fo Shan), across the street from a paper-cutting factory; **Sun Wui** (also Xin.Hui or Hsin Huei), with the best restaurant in town (but nothing exciting); **Kong Moon**; and **Toy Shan** (Tai Shan) as well as Canton. I am told a new ten-story hotel was built recently in Toy Shan and I saw the new extension to the one in Sun Wui being built. It looks nice. Generally speaking, these hotels in Kwangtung are drab—no carpets, of course—bare cement floors, mosquito nets, no air-conditioning, spittoons on the floor, no color. You're in the tropics here.

Oh, come on, you'll survive!

8
Food

The Chinese food visitors get is usually excellent. The secret of eating a Chinese meal is finding out first how many courses you will be getting. If there are twelve courses, take no more than one-twelfth of what you will usually eat in a meal from each plate; otherwise, you will be too full to eat any of the later dishes. Also take your time. You can't rush through a big meal.

To get started on a dish, you will notice your Chinese hosts putting food on the plates of the people around them. You can do this too if you want. For other tips on etiquette, see Chapter 9.

No need to worry about "Chinese restaurant syndrome"—its symptoms are an increased, stronger pulse, and a tight feeling around the sinuses. This "syndrome" is a result of the large amount of monosodium glutamate that Chinese cooks in North America put in their food. Cooks in China use a little—but not so much.

Travelers in the care of Luxingshe have found their meals ready for them—no need to order. The nice thing about a Chinese meal is the variety. If you don't like one thing, there is always something else you might have. If you do have food preferences, do let your Responsible Person know. You might even want to discuss with him the elaborateness of the accommodations when meat and rice for the common man is rationed, if indeed this bothers you.

TIPS ON ORDERING

If you have to do your own ordering, here are some guidelines. Menus in hotels for Foreign Friends usually are in English and Chinese.

1. Calculate one dish for each person, then add rice and one more dish. For two people, order three dishes plus rice. For five people, order six dishes plus rice. This will give you abundance. If you find you are getting too much, order less.

2. Every restaurant has its specialties—dishes the chefs are especially good at, using local ingredients. If you are near a lake or ocean, it'll be fresh fish or crab. So ask the waiter what the specialty of the house is. Order it a day in advance if necessary. (See Chapter 19, Useful Chinese Phrases.)

It is more interesting to eat in a large group so there will be a great variety of dishes. When ordering for many people, choose one poultry, one pork, one beef, one fish, one vegetable, with soup at the end. If you need more courses, start the rounds again—if you've already chosen chicken, then choose duck or goose. Vary the tastes and textures: sweet, pepper hot, salty, steamed, deep fried, stir fried, poached or boiled, roasted, baked in mud—the variety is endless. (See Chapter 19, Useful Chinese Phrases.)

4. Tea drinking is an art in China; some springs are famous for their tea-making qualities. If you do get to Hangchow, try Lung Ching tea there. A black tea such as Keemun is good in the wintertime and when you're having greasy foods. Lu An tea should help you sleep. Oolong is the most common tea in south China, while most foreigners like jasmine tea, the sweet-scented tea with bits of jasmine petals in it. If you have an upset stomach—or cankers in the mouth—try Hung Pean (chrysanthemum tea) from Chekiang, sweetened with sugar.

5. Don't feel that every meal must be a banquet. If you're adventurous, you might try one of the food stalls or noodle shops at lunch time. If you're not feeling well, you can order rice congee—rice cooked to a gruel consistency and served with a bit of flavoring (salted egg, fermented bean curd, salt fish). This is easy on the stomach. You could avoid the fried dishes, or order a boiled egg.

6. Don't look for chop suey or chow mein with crispy noodles or fortune cookies—these are American dishes. There are fried noodles in China, but they are not the same as in the United States.

7. For desserts, Foreign Friends will be offered Western-style sweet pastries and fruits—bananas, apples, pears, oranges, and pineapples. If you're in Kwangtung in May and June, ask for fresh lichees. Also ask for pomelo (boo look), a sweet grapefruit with a thick rind. China also has coffee shop-type sweets, ice cream, another form of ice cream with black beans, and sweet pastries.

8. In addition to tea, you can order wine and beer with meals, and nonalcoholic drinks such as orange soda, milk, and coffee. Some Chinese like to mix their beer with the orange soda.

9. In hotels for Foreign Friends, you will be given a choice of Chinese or Western breakfasts. The Chinese breakfast will depend on where you are at the time. In the south, you could get *dim sum* (little meat pastries, fried or steamed), or rice congee with peanuts, pickles, or salted eggs. In the north, you could get small meat dishes and vegetables, or "oil sticks" (like foot-long dough-nuts)—deep fried and delicious, but hard to digest. In Shanghai you might get fermented gelatinous rice balls with sugar inside. Or you might get baked buns with sweet bean paste inside.

Western breakfast could be fried or scrambled eggs, toast, coffee, canned orange juice or canned peaches.

WESTERN FOOD

This is available but naturally is not as good as the Chinese. Bread is frequently brown, but sometimes white. Traveling delegations usually get Chinese food at first, but toward the end of their visit get a Western meal.

Don't worry if you don't use chopsticks. Forks will be provided in hotels for Foreign Friends.

For a change to Western fare, you might try the Seamen's Club, the Red House Café (formerly the Chez Louis), or the Overseas Chinese Hotel, all in **Shanghai**; or the International Club in **Peking**. One traveler pointed out the excellent Western food on the **Sian-Shanghai train**; in fact, all the food on that train was great.

One American newsman says, "You can get lemon pie on Nanking Road near the Cathay Hotel in Shanghai, but don't let it fall on your toe."

REGIONAL SPECIALTIES

In some specialty restaurants you can get Moslem food, vegetarian dishes, dog meat, snake, Peking duck, Mongolian hot pot, and other regional dishes (Mongolian hot pot is a cook-it-yourself soup of lamb meat, liver, kidneys, cabbage and rice noodles). An infinite variety of food is found, especially in Peking. Some restaurants recommended by visitors are:

In Peking:

Horn of Plenty (Shantung)
Mount Omei Restaurant (Szechuan—pepper hot)
Cheng-tu Restaurant (Szechuan)
Overseas Chinese Restaurant (Cantonese)
Peking Roast Duck Restaurant (on lane off Wang Fu
    Ching St. near Peking Hotel)

In Canton:

Yu I Restaurant (sweet cakes)
Pei Yuan Restaurant (dog)
Pan Chi (Cantonese)
Kwangchow Restaurant
Mongolian Hot Pot Restaurant
Wild Game Restaurant (tiger, snake, monkey, etc.)
Remin Restaurant (Hakka style—this is one of China's
    ethnic minorities)
Moslem Restaurant
Snake Restaurant

DINNER INVITATIONS

If you are invited by nonofficial Chinese friends, don't be surprised if they ask you to phone the restaurant and make the reservation. Most of the top restaurants are reserved for officials and foreigners. Sounds unfair? Ask your Responsible Person about it. I think it might have something to do with gourmet food being bourgeois and that there are a lot of foreigners in Peking, all wanting to try some of the best Chinese food in the world, and not enough restaurants.

Do have the hotel's Service Desk or your Responsible Person phone ahead for a reservation and discuss the menu. Otherwise you might have to wait an hour or more from the time you arrive before you eat.

My impression is that Chinese citizens eating at Overseas Chinese hotels have to pay grain ration coupons for their meal; if they are guests at hotels for Foreign Friends, they do not.

9
Local Customs

YOUR "RESPONSIBLE PERSON"

Most RPs are graduates of the Foreign Languages Institutes or the foreign language department of a university. Their jobs are assigned; they did not choose to be an RP. You can be assured that they have a high level of "political consciousness"—otherwise, they would not be allowed to work so closely with foreigners. When you question them, you will get the party line.

Some RPs are excellent, dependable, and efficient. Some are fresh out of school, so they may not know the ropes yet, or the technical jargon that some visitors demand. So please be patient if they have trouble understanding and translating. Some have only two years of language training. But most will make every effort to help meet your requests and needs.

For most visitors, the RP who travels with you will be the Chinese you get to know best of all. He has probably read all about you and discussed your itinerary with his director and your host organization. The decision is not his if some of your special requests are rejected.

Sometimes your RP is not allowed to eat with you in hotels, even on tour. He is certainly not allowed to accept tips and gifts. (See section on Etiquette, below.) Although I have felt very close to some when we were together in China, I have never received any answers to my letters, not even thank-yous for photographs I sent, from any RP. I have heard of only one visitor receiving a letter from an RP, so don't feel slighted if you don't hear from him after your return home.

Large tour groups may have two RPs or itinerary coordinators who travel with them, and additional interpreters are obtained in each city.

Your RP is your link to your host organization. Keep him happy by your punctuality, cooperation, and friendliness, and he will do his best for you.

"NO"—WHAT IT MEANS AND SHOULD YOU TRY TO ARGUE?

You will have to judge for yourself when a negative decision should be challenged. Ross Terrill was told he couldn't go swimming but insisted on it anyway, and his escorts didn't mind. The reason was concern for his safety, and when he survived, everything was hunky-dory. Can you imagine how embarrassed the Chinese would be if an honored guest drowned!

I found that by protesting to a hotel clerk who said there was no room, I did get one. I also found that I could get permission to see the arts and crafts exhibit at the Trade Fair, after the Service Desk told me "no."

You can try arguing in Chinese terms; if a telegraph clerk refuses to accept your cable in English, look at her indignantly and remind her to "serve the people."

Ross Terrill once wanted to go for a walk but his companions objected that it wasn't safe. "But . . . China is the 'safest country on earth!'. . ." he argued, successfully.

This does not mean you should try to argue every time you are told "It is not convenient," or "Your safety cannot be guaranteed." It could mean (1) language is a problem and they don't understand your request; (2) they don't want to be bothered trying; (3) they don't want too many people going there but if you insist, they'll let you go; (4) there is genuine concern for your safety; or (5) you really are not allowed, and as a good guest, you should accept their decision gracefully. If you are a bad guest, do you think they'll cooperate fully with you—or let you come back?

If you really feel frustrated, send a postcard home telling what an awful time you are having because they won't let you photograph the Forbidden City in the moonlight, or whatever. Who knows? It might work, since outgoing mail is also examined.

ASK QUESTIONS

An official of the Overseas Chinese Travel Service once told me visitors should "ask questions." It was the only advice he had for foreigners.

It is good advice. For some reason, the Chinese do not volunteer much information. If they did, you wouldn't need this guidebook. When in doubt, ask!

ETIQUETTE

You will frequently be greeted by **handclapping** as a sign of welcome and appreciation at institutions and cultural performances. It might even happen on the streets. The normal response is to clap back.

You may be asked for **criticisms and suggestions**. Individuals respond to this differently. I feel if you have them, then give them; but don't go on about how things are done in North America. That doesn't apply to China. Criticisms should be helpful in the context of a developing country. Frequently criticisms and suggestions by visitors are brought up later at staff meetings, discussed, and acted upon.

You can reciprocate by asking your hosts a similar question about your country.

Hotel Wastebaskets:

You have probably read about old tennis shoes and torn socks abandoned in hotel wastebaskets being rushed to their owners by a panting service comrade on a bicycle just before the train pulls out of the station.

This happens so frequently (but don't count on it) that it might be wise to have your Responsible Person tell the service comrade that you don't want what you leave in the wastebasket. Under *no circumstance,* I repeat, do *not* tell the service comrade he can have it. Tell him you don't have room for it. If all else fails, take it graciously and try to get rid of it later in a public trash bin at the station.

Every traveler will have a wastebasket story. Maybe you can top this one, but an American businessman at the Tung-fang hotel in 1974 got back the paper clip he left behind when he was there in 1973. You may have your own interpretation, but I think the Chinese are fanatics about giving an impression of honesty to foreigners; I never had any trouble getting rid of junk at the Overseas Chinese hotels. I also think the Chinese are so used to being thrifty themselves that they cannot understand why anyone would throw away a sock that could be mended or a shoe that could be fixed. Besides, years of accepting used clothing during the war has resulted in an overreaction. They are proud people.

Tipping:

As I explained before, tipping is insulting to people who want to "serve the people," and you risk getting an angry retort if you attempt it. Service is the norm, and you will find most service comrades cheerfully willing to help without compensation even for such time-consuming tasks as long-distance phone calls. In the Canton Overseas Chinese Mansion, a list of what a service comrade will do is posted above the desk.

Of course, you may feel compelled to repay kindness especially to a friendly, competent Responsible Person who has traveled with you for three weeks. Just remember also that you may be jeopardizing your Responsible Person's job. If he is in the habit of accepting gifts, neighbors and colleagues will know about it and he may be called upon to explain the presence of foreign goods and unusual wealth. So don't feel hurt or act indignant if your offer is refused.

As I mentioned before, one visitor solved this problem by giving a large English dictionary to the whole Luxingshe staff. Luxingshe can probably only absorb one dictionary, but a gift of this impersonal nature might be more acceptable. You could ask your Responsible Person how Luxingshe would feel about being given a recording of readings from Charles Dickens or Bernard Shaw (both acceptable authors). You could have other friends going to China take it later; otherwise, you would never know if it had been received. You will probably not receive even a thank-you note.

Candice Bergen's group is the only one I know who has managed to get a Responsible Person to accept a present for her children. Maybe the Responsible Person later gave the gifts to a nursery. Maybe she kept them herself. It would be interesting to find out.

See section on Gifts, under What to Take in Chapter 4.

Good Manners:

Good manners at home are good manners anywhere. *Don't* litter. *Don't* take "souvenirs"—especially from any historical place, such as a rock from the Great Wall. *Don't* pick flowers in parks.

In most other Asian countries it is fashionable to be late. Not so in China, where groups of children may be outside in the rain waiting for your car so they can applaud as you arrive.

As you would in visiting any private home, show your appreciation by telling your host about the things you like and, if you can do it nicely, even the things you dislike.

One thing that embarrasses the Chinese was mentioned by John Burns, the resident correspondent for the Toronto *Globe and Mail* who wrote in April 1974: "It is a difficult thing for many **Western radicals** to accept, but it is an acknowledged fact that the Chinese are not par-

Lion (female) inside the Forbidden City, Peking.

Temple of Heaven, Peking.

Park in Canton.

Pandas in the Canton Zoo.

Girl on tractor, Ma chow commune, Shanghai.

Hoop dance performed by kindergarten class in Sun Wai.

A mother and child photographed in the village of Toy Shan.

Man with snakes in the village of Toy Shan.

ticularly interested in, and are even embarrassed by, foreigners who come to China determined to impress their hosts with their revolutionary fervor . . .

". . . the Chinese, nationalists before they are Communists, do not understand foreigners who run their own country down while abroad. They are made uncomfortable, moreover, by any attempt to enlist their assent to denunciation by a government with which China has friendly relations . . ."

Toasting:

Toasting at banquets is a complicated art in China, but you are not expected to know the finer points. Just do what you do at home. Stand, clink glasses, drink, and have a spokesman for your group respond in kind.

A frequent toast given by the Chinese is to the friendship of the world's people, the Chinese and the people of your country, and the health of the friends and comrades present.

Glasses are small and usually filled with *mao tai*, which is very potent. The spokesman for your group should respond, adding something about the occasion, your sadness about leaving China perhaps, and the new friends you have made, and wishing that you will all meet again in your country.

Toasts might continue all evening—so might the meal. If the banquet is extremely large, the host may want to circulate to all the tables, drinking toasts at each table.

On smaller, less formal occasions, the Chinese may want to drink you under the table. Be alert; they may be putting tea in their own glasses. You may want to try that one yourself after a while.

I have been to banquets where I haven't touched a drop of liquor (I can't get it past my nose—it's so strong) and I don't think I offended anyone. Maybe I get away with it because I'm a woman, but if you don't want to drink so much, try to divert them. Try exchanging songs. Ask them to teach you their songs. Try "The East Is Red"—you probably know the tune by now.

Giving a Banquet:

One way of returning hospitality, especially to a Responsible Person, is to give hospitality. If he persists in refusing your invitation to eat with you, he might relent and join you the day before you leave as a farewell gesture.

You may want to throw a banquet for some of your Chinese colleagues and people who have been particularly helpful. Discuss your guest list with your Responsible Person so you won't offend anyone important by leaving them out. Make sure the Responsible Person knows he's invited—with his spouse. If he still refuses, tell him you need help with protocol problems, customs, and interpreting.

Your Responsible Person will probably go with you to talk with the restaurant manager. Give the manager some guidelines as to costs and what special wines and dishes you would like. See the section on Food in Chapter 6 and also Chapter 8. Discuss ahead of time with your Responsible Person how the banquet will be paid for.

Your Responsible Person should be able to help with invitations and transportation for guests if needed. He can help you with place cards. Your guest of honor usually faces the door and sits to the left of the head of your group. Chinese banquet tables usually seat ten. At rectangular tables, the place of honor is the center of the long side of the table—again facing the door.

Unless you are with an official delegation, don't worry too much about protocol, though people do appreciate your efforts to be polite. If you have problems ask your guests what you should do about toasting. It makes a good topic of conversation.

Enjoy your banquet. It could go on for three or four hours. The guests usually make the first move to leave.

Flirting:

You may be tempted to flirt with a Chinese citizen of the opposite sex. Friendliness is appreciated, but anything beyond that may mean that you will be interviewed by the Public Security Office and asked why you have insulted a Chinese citizen. It could also mean that you will be on the next plane out of the country. There have been some marriages of Chinese with foreign residents, but usually after much discussion, and three weeks is not enough time.

You will note that even handholding is not very common; Chinese are more likely to socialize with members of their own sex than to pair off in public.

You will probably be considered uncivilized if you indulge in too much display of affection, even with your own spouse. The Chinese will be embarrassed.

WILL YOU BE FOLLOWED?

I think if the Chinese have any reason for suspecting you of subversion, you won't be allowed into the country. If you are already there, yes, you may be followed if they have any inkling that you'll do something wrong. In some cases, following you won't be necessary. Foreigners stand out so obviously that any suspicious movements will probably be reported by ordinary citizens to the Public Security Office anyway, and it would be easy to trace your movements later.

I have mentioned how one Chinese-American scholar was charged with subversion. He must have been watched for some time. I do know that one American businessman found he had a jogging partner when he took his morning run in Liuhua Park every day. This could be because the Chinese wanted to protect an important trade official—after all, he could fall and hurt himself. Your guess is as good as mine.

PHOTOGRAPHY

(See also What to Take in Chapter 4.)

If you wish to have your films processed in China, leave them with the service comrade in your hotel. It may take two to four days. Officially, you may take photographs anywhere except of military installations, on air planes and boats, and in the Peking subway. I was told I couldn't take photos of soldiers even on the street, but I did take pictures of individual members of the People's Liberation Army with their permission.

I would also avoid "Big Character Posters." In fact, some groups have been asked not to photograph them. During periods of intense revolutionary criticism, like the anti-Lin Piao and anti-Confucius campaigns, citizens write criticisms of their fellow workers, too, and post these where they can be read and discussed by other colleagues. Many of these posters are very private; perhaps we can compare them with what members of a sensitivity or therapy group say about each other. They are not for outsiders, so do not photograph them.

Please don't take flash photos at cultural performances. It disturbs the audience. This is my personal request. The Chinese may let you. Stage lighting is usually sufficient for black-and-white and fast color film. Do, however, ask if you can get right up next to the stage, and squat down—shooting with available light as professional photographers do. Flash shots from the middle of a theater rarely work anyway.

Individual citizens may object to your taking pictures of scenes unflattering to their nation. You could argue that "no one abroad will believe that everything is good and nothing is bad in China; so to convince them of the good, I have to show some of the bad. I mean no offense."

If all else fails, you might suggest calling a policeman and an interpreter (if you need one). I am told policemen are very reasonable about these matters. You may be detained and your motives questioned at great length. It might help if you offered to remove the film from your camera and give it to them.

If things still look grim, try to contact your embassy.

Among some groups of people like boat people, pedicab drivers, and peasants, there are still some who have superstitious fears of having their picture taken. So ask permission if you think they might object.

I found, however, that in my father's village many people asked me to take their picture. Of course I sent them a copy later, and, of course, I was known to them as a relative.

I have only had trouble once taking photos in China because I usually follow the rules. I have found one easy explanation is to tell them I am *wah que* or *hwa chiao*—Overseas Chinese. Usually this or a foreign face is sufficient.

WHEN YOU VISIT A COMMUNE, FACTORY, OR SCHOOL

You can expect to be greeted at the door by the director or applauding children. You will be taken first to a comfortable board room for introductions, tea, and a ten- to fifteen-minute briefing on the history, purpose, program, statistics, and government of the place.

There will be more than one person present representing the institution. These will probably be members of the Revolutionary Committee in charge, but ask if you are curious.

After the briefing, you will be given a chance to ask questions. Don't be surprised if the Chinese discuss their answers before responding. This is because a lot of policy is still in flux; decisions are made by committees. It is part of the process of involving many people in decision making.

You may be asked if there is something special you want to see. Try to avoid making this too complicated if you are in a large group. If you don't have time to ask all the questions you want, you may have an opportunity as you tour the premises. You can expect, in most cases where there are children, that you will have a performance of songs and dances about tractor drivers and loving Chairman Mao.

Visits to institutions are usually two to three hours long. If you want to present a souvenir gift or take a group photo, inform your Responsible Person in advance, so time will be allotted. Sometimes you will be taken back to the board room and asked for criticism and suggestions (see section on Etiquette, above)—or you will go directly back to your bus or car. The children will probably be lined up at the gate to clap as you leave.

Some visitors are at a loss when asked if they have any questions. If this is your problem, read the section in Chapter 12 on Ask Questions, Observe, Absorb, Ponder.

LOOKING UP SPECIFIC CHINESE CITIZENS AND RESIDENTS

As a courtesy to your Responsible Person, do inform him if you want to take time off from your scheduled tour to visit with friends or relatives. You might ask him when the best time would be for you to meet with them. I have taken local Chinese with me on trips to communes and schools, and you could ask to do the same if there is room in your bus.

Local Chinese may go to your hotel to see you, but may have to ask permission before entering, giving your name and showing their I.D. cards. In some hotels, they have to present their permission slip to the Service Desk on your floor for stamping; in other hotels, you will have to sign their permission slip. Procedures differ. If they are uneasy about seeing you in the hotel, you could arrange to meet in a restaurant, a park, or their home. (See also Are You Worried About Going? under Overseas Chinese in Chapter 2.)

In many cases, particularly if you are a Foreign Friend, the Chinese you expect to see will first be checked out by the authorities to verify your relationship to them. In some cases, before meeting you they will discuss what they should talk about, and after your meeting they will discuss what you talked about. Do not persist in asking questions that a Chinese seems reluctant to answer. Do not expect any spontaneous rap sessions. I once asked a friend what happened to his family during the Cultural Revolution, and was bluntly but politely told it was none of my business.

The relatives of Overseas Chinese are also visited by the authorities before your visit is approved, and for the same reasons; but beyond this, unless there is reason to suspect something is wrong, I feel Overseas Chinese have a freer time fraternizing with Chinese citizens.

I have visited many Chinese homes accompanied only by my relatives and occasionally alone. No complications that I know of. Of course, the Overseas Chinese Travel Service was aware of who my relatives were. If they wanted to know what people I visited they could ask my relatives.

On the other hand, a Chinese-American scholar told me the Overseas Chinese Travel Service arranged some of his interviews for him, and for these, an interpreter was always present, even though he didn't need one. Sometimes when the Chinese-American tried to arrange his own interviews, the local scholar said it would be better to arrange the visit through the Travel Service. Some interviews he arranged entirely on his own. I don't know if there is any connection, but this Chinese-American later had his papers confiscated and was accused of spying.

In 1973 I had a letter of introduction to Prince Sihanouk of Cambodia, a resident of Peking, but the Overseas Chinese Travel Service refused to even check to see if an appointment could be arranged. "He's too busy," my Responsible Person told me. They also unsuccessfully tried for hours to find a Chinese scientific organization I wanted to contact, though I know other foreigners have visited it. I got the impression that the problem was bureaucratic. The Overseas Chinese Travel Service is not used to this kind of request. On my next trip, maybe I'll try the Foreign Ministry Information Office as all the other journalists do.

As an Overseas Chinese, you can usually visit your "native place," the place your family originally came from, particularly if it is in Kwangtung province or a main city like Peking or Shanghai. Some visit Fukien province, but few visit west China. If you cannot visit your family, some members may be sent to visit you in Peking or Canton.

HINTS WHEN VISITING LOCAL CHINESE

If accompanied by a Chinese friend or relative, I would avoid buying anything in a store because he may want to pay for it. The cash salary range for most people in the south is from about ¥15 to ¥130 a month. Most city people, even doctors, get about ¥40 to ¥75. Salaries in the north are slightly higher.

Of course, rent is low, a Chinese doesn't have to pay exorbitant medical bills if he is sick, and he pays no income tax. But he has to save a long time to buy what you wouldn't think twice about buying.

Hospitality may demand that you be given a gift. Be gracious and suggest something inexpensive like a poster if you are asked. See section on Etiquette.

I have visited many homes—of peasants, officials, workers, and professional people. By Western standards, they are crowded. One professional couple with two

99

children might have one or two tiny bedrooms—period. They would share a kitchen and bathroom with several other families. In only rare cases will there be room for overnight guests, especially in the cities.

Toilets are the squatting kind. In smaller communities, you may find a container of earth or a bucket of water for covering or flushing.

In rural areas, you might have to sight-see on foot or on the hard back ends of bicycles, since there may not be any other means of transportation. It is a real adventure!

KEEPING IN TOUCH WITH THE NEWS

In China, you're in another world—you may feel you're on another planet. There's no Walter Cronkite, no Toronto *Star,* no *Time* and *Newsweek.* The foreign ministry's excerpts from foreign wire services are not generally available. Foreigners can buy some but *not all* Chinese newspapers. Besides, who has time to read Chinese after a hard day of sight-seeing? Even if you can read Chinese, Chinese editors have a different philosophy of what to put in newspapers than ours do.

In Peking, one good source if you have time is to see if your embassy has newspapers from home. These may be very old, however. Maybe the embassy will let you see the foreign ministry's excerpts.

The best solution is to have a good shortwave radio. In Peking, you can usually get news from Voice of America and the British Broadcasting Corporation. In the south, you can get Radio Australia and Radio Hong Kong in addition. News is usually every hour on the hour and bands are listed in the section on What to Take in Chapter 4.

IF YOU GET SICK

China is among the healthiest and cleanest countries of Asia. You will find few flies in the big cities. The streets are swept several times a day and the hotels are mopped several times also.

Standard practice in Asia is to eat only cooked food and to drink boiled water. Animal and human excrement is used as fertilizer.

You will note in Canton that there are no screens on the windows. If you are bothered by mosquitoes, use the net above your bed. You can also burn incense coils that keep mosquitoes away.

Canton attempts several times during the mosquito season to fumigate the entire city with DDT. The occasions are rather festive, and go on for about two hours in the evening. People are put out of the hotels and wait in the parks or on the street—at least, that's what happened in 1973.

Cities farther north don't seem to have a mosquito problem.

Medical facilities are excellent. Many Overseas Chinese go to China for acupuncture treatment. I met a lady from Indonesia in Shanghai for heart surgery, and James Reston of *The New York Times* successfully had his appendix removed.

If visitors are sick, it is usually because of a virus (from Hong Kong, of course!)—mainly, the common cold. If you are sick, your Responsible Person can arrange for you to see a doctor. If you are sick at night in your hotel, contact the Service Desk. If you have a language problem, point to the phrase you need in the Useful Phrases.

101

You will probably be given a choice of Western or traditional Chinese medicine or both. The usual antibiotic is Tetracycline. Chinese herbal medicines are effective and have no side effects. Chinese hospitals are up to Western standards except for one thing—the price. Your Blue Cross won't believe it if you bother to make a claim. My daughter had a cold treated by a commune doctor. There was no charge. In Canton, an office visit cost us two and a half cents; a two-day supply of cough medicine and antibiotics cost us fifty-two cents.

The Chinese are usually very concerned about the health of their guests. They frequently check whether you have enough clothes on for various kinds of weather. If you are a chronic complainer about your health, you might get a doctor even if you don't request it.

If you are still worried about health, read Dr. Victor Sidel's book, *Serve the People.* He will tell you how China has eliminated most diseases.

IF YOU GET INTO TROUBLE

Chances are a thousand to one that these things won't happen, but just in case . . .

If You Run Out of Money:

Ask your embassy to cable home for some. It takes five banking days. Or borrow from fellow travelers. See section on Finances in Chapter 4.

Hostile Crowds:

If you *think* you're surrounded by a hostile crowd—try smiling at them. Chances are they're just curious. In Shanghai, they will surround your car five-deep and stare. Pointing your camera at them will make them fall back only for a moment—so don't bother trying that. Besides, a camera might antagonize them. Try making friends. Speak to them quietly, in English if you don't know Chinese. Someone may understand. Above all, smile and act friendly.

If you do find yourself alone in a hostile crowd—try to find out why they are hostile. The Chinese do not usually get angry at foreigners because they are foreigners, not even at Japanese, the hated enemy for so many years.

It is probably something you have done that has upset them—and it's usually taking pictures of the wrong places (see section on Photography, above) or flirting.

Try not to lose your temper; keep cool, polite, friendly. Keep apologizing. Quote Chairman Mao. Talk about the friendship of the Chinese people and the people of your country.

Demonstrations:

Don't be afraid of them. They are usually orderly. The blond wife of one foreign correspondent used to wave at marching demonstrators with a big friendly grin on her face. Participants used to be so surprised by this, they'd break step, stare, and grin back. If you don't believe me, read Colin McCullough's *Stranger in China.*

Car Accidents:

If your car accidentally injures a Chinese, do what you would in your own country. Give first aid, and then get him quickly to a doctor or a hospital. You may want to extend your sympathies to the family of the injured and discuss with your Responsible Person and your embassy whether or not you should give a financial contribution to the family of the victim.

Breaking the Law:

If you are accused of breaking a Chinese law, try to contact your embassy. Don't expect the kind of justice known in the West. There is no habeas corpus; there are no lawyers. You may be shipped out of the country; you may be jailed until your government can negotiate for your release.

Read *Prisoner of Mao* before you consider taking in drugs or smuggling contraband. It tells what Chinese prisons are like.

10
Transportation

PLANES

There are a couple of flights a day between major cities. Some are direct in the big new jets (the trip from Peking to Canton takes three hours, Peking to Nanking two hours, and Peking to Shanghai slightly less than two hours). Some are very small propeller planes and take all day. In the winter, the smaller, older planes may be extremely cold. Be sure to ask which one you are going on.

On planes, announcements are made in Chinese and English over the loudspeaker. No cameras, binoculars, or radio receivers are allowed to be used on board. If you choose the candy the service comrade gives you, you can eat the paper stuck to it. It's made of rice. Don't expect a meal. Be at the airport on time, but don't expect your flight to be always on time. Planes won't fly in bad weather and if there's any doubt about maintenance. The result is an extremely low accident rate.

TRAINS

The fare is slightly less than plane for a "soft" class seat, considerably less for "hard" class. Soft-class berths are more expensive than plane fares. Soft class is the height of bourgeois comfort; we had clean pink slip covers with lace doilies, lace curtains, a table with a potted plant, and a compartment for two of us that was meant for four. The service was excellent and we even had "Russian" food in the dining car.

"Hard" class really has four to a compartment, and the seats are hard.

BOATS AND BUSES

You can also travel by boat, which is pleasant if you like boats, or by public bus, which is an interesting experience if you are in good shape.

Overseas Chinese may have a choice between a boat and a bus south of Canton. I would recommend the boat. On overnight boats, passengers are given a sleeping space on a platform with about eleven other people. Bedding can be rented for a few cents. Try to get one of the newer boats. They are less noisy and more spacious. No privacy, of course, but think of it as an adventure, an opportunity to meet and see ordinary people relaxing.

Day boats are more crowded. You sit on a platform and, if you are lucky, you can lean up against a wall. They are slower and less crowded than public buses.

If you are wealthy, you can also hire a taxi for out-of-town trips.

LOCAL TRANSPORTATION

Some cities have bicycle rickshaws and scooter rickshaws. Prices are fixed and fares are paid in advance at the rickshaw stand. Bicycle rickshaws cost very little but you can go only short distances. Since few drivers know English, be sure to have your destination written down beforehand in Chinese characters.

Taxi fares are usually calculated according to the odometer. There are no taxi meters. In some places you can hire rickshaws or taxis on an hourly basis, and since they are in short supply, you may want to have your taxi wait for you at several stops.

It is usually difficult to get a taxi except at a hotel. Even then, in Peking and Canton I've had to wait up to an hour to get one. Better have the Service Desk in the lobby book you one a day in advance, particularly for Sunday. In Shanghai, however, I found a taxi stand in an ordinary neighborhood.

Public Buses:

These are usually very crowded, especially during the early morning and late afternoon, and all day Sunday. But they may be your only means of transport. Try them if you are athletic or adventurous, or during an off-hour. Hotel personnel can tell you which bus to take, or take a map with you and point. Fellow passengers are helpful. The ticket taker is usually near the rear door—so if it's too crowded to get near her, you can pass your fare to the person next to you in that direction, or else wait until you get off and hand it to her through the window.

Do not be surprised if the natives get up and offer

you their seats. It is Chinese courtesy, but do consider that many people have been working long hours and then also attending meetings. On the other hand, if you refuse, they may feel uncomfortable having an honored guest standing. Take your pick.

Subway:

In Peking, you may also want to try the subway. Ask your Responsible Person if you can visit it and the air raid tunnels under the city.

11
Shopping and Friendship Stores

ARTS AND CRAFTS

China is famous for its arts and crafts, though one American businessman told me the best carvers and weavers are in Hong Kong. But look around and judge for yourself. Compare prices. I keep hearing stories about travelers who paid one-tenth the U.S. price for a tea set, or one-twentieth the Hong Kong price on scrolls.

The Chinese are very honest in their business dealings, but frequently the clerk may not know what good quality is. So thoroughly check the pieces you want to buy. As with all handmade goods, no two pieces are alike.

China still produces arts and crafts with traditional themes, although occasionally you will find a few carvings of workers and peasants among the feudal ladies and goddesses. The Chinese know what people abroad want to buy.

The nonbusiness shopper could ask to see the arts and crafts section of the Trade Fair, but prices there are quoted only to businessmen ordering in commercial quantities, and display items may be for display only, and not available anywhere. But a trip to the Fair. is worthwhile to see the beautiful things that you might look for elsewhere.

The best buys for arts and crafts are not the Friendship Stores, but the Chinese equivalent of the "factory outlets," frequently but not always found in the cities where the goods are made. Transportation costs are not added and the variety is usually better. Ask to see the factories where they make the items you are interested in. It will add to the sentimental value of the goods if you can say you saw them being made. Ask a local guide or the Service Desk of the hotel where you can buy the local products listed.

Ivory carvings: Canton and Peking
Porcelain: Chingteh County in Kiangsi; Swatow in Kwangtung (north of Canton); Liling in Hunan (Changsha might be the closest you can get to it)
Ceramics: Fat Shan (just outside Canton); Shihwan in Kwangtung
Painted Clay Figures: Wusih in Kiangsu
Cloisonné, painted bottles, soapstone carving, lacquer: Peking
Lacquer: Chienchow in Fukien
Jade: Peking and Shanghai
Wood Carvings: Chekiang province
Silk: Hangchow (This is where those famous woven "photographs" are made.) Canton and Soochow
Embroidery: Swatow and Soochow
Silk Brocades: jackets, housecoats, etc., Shanghai
Table cloths: Shanghai, Swatow, and Tsingtao in Shangtung
Fur pieces: Shanghai and Peking
Rugs: Peking and Tientsin

Pictures: (made of sea shells, bird feathers, and cork) Peking and Sian

ANTIQUES

If you're after antiques, each city has stores for them, but be sure you get a signed receipt of purchase and a red wax seal attached to the antique. Otherwise, you will not be able to get it out of the country.

As with antique stores everywhere, you have to know what to look for if you want a bargain. If it is a non-Chinese antique, the Chinese pricers may not know the value and you may get a whopping good buy. Chinese antiques are not cheap, so unless you know quality, buy what you like. Remember the Chinese will not allow anything out of the country that is older than about 100 years; and the Americans and Canadians will only allow in, duty-free, items that are older than 100 years. Not much latitude there! Better check this with Luxingshe.

In Peking, you will find antique dealers on Liu Li Chang street and along Wang Fu Ching. There are also other shops with luxury-type goods for foreigners. Nagel's and Fodor's guides have good lists of Peking shops. There are also antique dealers in most large cities, so ask about them.

SHOPPING TIPS

1. Watercolor paintings on scrolls are good buys—especially those by obscure but good painters of the Ching dynasty.

2. If you know good value, you can still buy bargain jewelry. One friend swears she paid U.S. $75 for a gold

ring that would have cost her $500 in the United States.

3. Beware of wood or lacquer. If these are not properly dried, they will crack in overheated North American buildings.

4. Luxingshe or other host organizations will act as transfer agent if you want to ship large-sized purchases home. After you pay for your purchase at any store, be sure to get a receipt listing height, length, depth, weight, and value. Give this receipt to your host organization, which will calculate your shipping costs, bill you accordingly, and issue a bill of lading to you.

You may mail out smaller purchases yourself but these may be opened and inspected by the post office when you buy your stamps. Prohibited for export are such things as antiques without the red wax seal attached and some printed matter published before the Cultural Revolution.

5. Jades and antiques are expensive. The period of giveaway prices in such Chinese handicrafts is over. But you can still get bargains if you have a good eye.

6. The best jade pieces are multicolored ones in which the carver has worked the different colors into the design. Then you can be sure you have something truly unique. Jade jewelry is said to be better in Hong Kong; but Hong Kong abounds in phony jade, so the problem there is finding a reliable dealer.

7. China does not mass market the way America does. There are no "national brands" in handicrafts. The things you see available in Canton may not be found in Peking. So buy what you like when you see it. You may not see it again.

8. When you're comparing prices with North America, don't forget to calculate the rate of duty and the shipping costs if these apply. (See also Comparison Shopping in Chapter 4.)

9. SAVE YOUR SALES SLIPS, so you can argue with customs in your own country. They will be in Chinese with English numbers, so make a note on them of what each slip is for.

10. Store hours are usually 8 A.M. to 8:30 P.M. daily, but some stores are closed during the day, opening only during the early morning and early evening.

NOVELTIES

If your speed, like mine, is not in the $3,000 rug range, China does have a good variety of novelties, things distinctively Chinese and even revolutionary for U.S. $6 or less. These you can take back to your nieces and nephews and bridge buddies. Most of the following are obtainable from Friendship Stores:

Acupuncture Dolls:

These are about ten inches high, with genuine acupuncture needles and an instruction booklet (in Chinese). The best ones are from Shanghai pharmacies—together about U.S.$6. If that's too expensive, then there are the **acupuncture posters** found in bookstores—cheap.

Posters:

Some in the old Chinese landscape tradition, where nature predominates and man is tiny. But look closely and you'll see smoke from factory chimneys, and power lines. In 1973, these were less than U.S. five cents. Then there are the revolutionary posters, pictures of Chairman

Mao, movie stills, soldiers, workers and peasants—some day these will be collector's items.

Postcards:

In sets. These are not just of cities but archeological finds, handicrafts, movie stills, etc.

Comic Books:

Read in China by both children and adults. Even though these are entirely in Chinese you can usually follow the plots.

Postage Stamps:

In sets. China produces some beautiful ones. You can also buy these at post offices. Put several sets on an envelope and send them home so you'll have the Chinese postmark.

Maps:

Of the world, showing China in the center. Maps of Canada and the United States in Chinese.

Books:

For children, there are books showing Chinese characters with equivalent pictures, like our ABCs.

If you're in a foreign-language bookstore, you'll find a great many books in English (cheap), all printed by the Foreign Languages Press in Peking. They make great souvenirs.

Miscellaneous:

Then there are those charming **paper cuttings**, **kites** with Chinese designs, traditional **baby bonnets** of silk or rayon, trimmed with fur ears to make baby look like a tiger kitten, **Mao caps**, **plastic eggs** with moving chicks inside, folding **scissors** and folding **fruit knives**.

There are fancy gold-trimmed **chopsticks** from Foochow and lovely metal-tipped chopsticks from Hangchow, **sandalwood fans** from Hangchow, and old **stone seals** (chops) found in the markets rather than the Friendship Stores. You can have a rubber stamp made of your name (if you can write the Chinese), with a fancy stone handle.

There are **oil paints** and Chinese **brushes and inks**. In fact, if you're into Chinese painting and want your works mounted on rice paper scrolls, Jung-pao-chai of Peking is "still the best in the world." Mounting here is cheaper than in Hong Kong; in 1973, a large scroll mounting cost U.S. $7.50. Other stores mount pictures more cheaply but not as well.

Some visitors recommend Chinese **wines and vodka**—U.S. ninety cents for a fifth in 1974. Or genuine Lung Ching **tea**—the best is grown in Hangchow. Overseas Chinese who know about these things might want to take home Chinese herbs and medicines. One Foreign Friend swears the Chinese herbal cure for colds beats anything you can get at home, and recommends it.

FRIENDSHIP STORES

These are set up so that foreigners won't have to buck curious crowds in ordinary stores. There is one in

115

every major city, and taxi drivers will know where they are. Prices are about the same as in other Chinese stores, but you can buy things there that you cannot find elsewhere because high quality, luxury-class items are only for export or the Friendship Stores.

Local Chinese are not usually allowed into these stores, and you will need your passport with its visa from a Chinese embassy abroad to get in. A Hong Kong entry permit won't do unless you are in a tour group. The Friendship Store in Peking is the best stocked, I found. There you can buy television sets, radios, watches, bicycles, sewing machines, arts and crafts, cosmetics, Chinese herbal medicines, canned or powdered milk, jewelry, thermos bottles, electric fans, cashmere sweaters, silk blouses and shirts.

You do not have to use ration coupons in the Friendship Stores, but if you are buying elsewhere, coupons are necessary for that good, cheap cotton most people wear. No coupon is necessary for other kinds of materials. While I know of one Overseas Chinese who was able to bully a Canton sales clerk into giving him a shirt without a coupon, it is not predictable. If you find you have to buy clothes because of lost luggage or unexpected weather, ask your Responsible Person or the Service Desk at your hotel for coupons.

An Overseas Chinese can buy things from the Friendship Store for local Chinese friends and relatives.

There is no haggling in China; prices are fixed and the same at both the tiny sidewalk stalls and the big department stores. Generally speaking, I found the quality and variety of goods in Shanghai stores better than elsewhere in China.

CUSTOMS

You will have no trouble with customs in Hong Kong, but if you go home through countries not friendly with China, your new possessions and especially printed materials may be confiscated. An American couple who went home in 1971 from Peking via the Trans-Siberian Railway had all their Chinese purchases seized at the Soviet border and returned to them in a sealed bag stamped "not to be opened in the Soviet Union."

You can manage something like that in other countries. If you think they'll seize your Chinese comic books and acupuncture charts, ask the customs to hold one suitcase "in bond" at your port of entry. They'll give it back to you, uninspected, when you leave.

Your big customs problem will be in your own country if you have exceeded your duty-free exemption. Generally speaking, U.S. citizens have a duty-free exemption of $100 on accompanied baggage. There are also exemptions for such things as printed matter, works of art (i.e., one of a kind), one quart of alcoholic beverages, and antiques (you will need proof of age). Everything else is taxable. In 1974, rates were higher for Chinese goods than for products from most other countries because China was not a "most favored nation" trading partner of the United States.

If you are going to make big purchases, check the rate with the U.S. Customs before you go. In 1974, bone china dinnerware, for example, was taxed at 50 percent to 70 percent of its value, folding screens with mother-of-pearl inlay at 33 percent to 50 percent, ivory carvings at 35 percent, jade carvings at 50 percent, and jewelry at 80 percent to 110 percent of the price the customs officer thought it was worth. But if you can prove something is "one of a kind," then it's free.

China is in a "most favored nation" trading category with Canada so the duty rate is the same as with most other countries. Canadians also have a $100 exemption. Canada also has a 12 percent federal sales tax calculated on the cost of the product plus the duty. Some Canadian duty rates (1974) were: ivory and jade carvings—15 percent; porcelain vases or silk in pieces—20 percent; jewelry—25 percent plus 10 percent excise tax; silk and cotton clothing—25 percent; linen, cotton, and fur pieces—22½ percent; fiction—10 percent.

Textbooks and antiques are free. You need a certificate to prove your antique is over 100 years old, obtainable—so says the Canadian Customs—from the British Antique Dealers' Association, Ltd., at 20 Rutland Gate, London S.W. 7, England, or from the Art and Antique Dealers League of America, Inc., at 807 Lexington Avenue, New York, N.Y. 10022. Also acceptable are approved associations in France, Belgium, the Netherlands, and Switzerland. But Canadian Customs does not say how you can take your antique to one of these associations if you are not going through that country.

The U.S. Customs booklet says "proof of antiquity obtained from the seller."

Customs payments really are relative to the customs officer doing the evaluating. Some are easier than others. Always apply your $100 exemption to possessions that carry the highest rate of duty. That way, an American can save $80 in duty on $100's worth of jewelry; he would save only $50 on $100 worth of jade carvings. And do consult your diplomatic missions abroad if you have questions.

12
What Is There
to See and Do?

WALK

Walk especially early in the morning before breakfast, when you are fresh (if you are fresh in the morning), before your Responsible Person comes to take you on your tour. Walk slowly without a camera, for cameras tend to separate people; they keep you from feeling, from savoring the waking of a world that is unlike any other on earth.

Life swims around you; people in parks doing ethereal *tai chi chuan* exercises in slow motion; store fronts open onto the street—wait—maybe they're tiny factories or homes with workshops in front; people hurrying to work on bicycles, buses, or trucks. "The East Is Red" plays on the loudspeakers.

China is one of the few countries of the world untouched by America, so look for the differences. There are no Coca-Cola signs here. In 1973, the bright-red billboards welcomed visitors, or exhorted "We all love Peking's Tien An Men!" and urged self-reliance, or condemned Confucius and Lin Piao.

China is politically oriented. Its mass media sell "right political thinking" and picture muscular, happy peasants, workers, and soldiers. It is a developing country, a poor country—but one that throbs with vitality. There are signs of its ancient civilization everywhere. Look for the old—remains of shrines and temples, carvings on the outside of tiny, wooden shops and old houses in Peking, "coolies" pulling heavy carts through the streets, little girls taking care of baby brothers strapped on their backs, bound feet on some of the very old women.

Look for the new—the shoes on the coolies, the fat healthy cheeks of little children, the cleanliness of the streets, the lack of beggars. Listen to the language; it is tonal. Cantonese especially sounds like singing on its nine-tone scale. Look at the writing—each character based on pictures, words made of philosophical concepts, not sounds.

People stare at foreign faces. They are not used to them. Smile back.

ASK QUESTIONS, OBSERVE, ABSORB, PONDER

For many travelers, studying a way of life and not just the monuments and the exoticisms is a new experience. What do you look for? What questions can you ask?

If you are at a loss when asked for questions, then you didn't do your homework before you left. You didn't find out about schools, factories, and farms in your own country, because if you did, you would want to compare.

Now that you're in China, you might want to do a

couple of surveys. Ask people how many children they
have and at what age they got married (to see how the
birth control program is working); or how many jobs
they had before this one and how old they are or have
they always lived in the same place? (how mobile are
they?); or ask which members of their family all live in
the same house or apartment and which do not (to see if
family units are being destroyed); or ask city people if
they have ever worked in a commune, for how long, and
what did they do?

The following list of questions is not an examina-
tion. In some cases there are no answers. I mention these
to stimulate your observations and thinking about
China. If you can't answer them, and your curiosity has
been aroused, then ask someone. Discuss the questions
in your group.

1. What actually happens during a criticism session,
how do they differ from a sensitivity or group therapy
session, and how would you compare the goals?

2. How much choice does the individual Chinese
have in regard to his job, his housing, his spouse, his
travel in China and abroad, etc.? How much choice did he
have in pre-Liberation days, and would China have
progressed since Liberation if China did not have its
controls?

3. What controls are there in China? Why no jewelry? No lipstick? No premarital sex? No general dis-
tribution of foreign periodicals? No unsupervised travel
abroad? Few marriages until the late twenties?

4. At what age does a child start to participate in the
decision-making process of the masses? How does he
learn to "serve the people"?

5. As you travel about the countryside, can you
estimate the percentage of human-operated irrigation

pumps as compared to motorized irrigation pumps? Do you think machines are really cheaper than human labor in China's situation?

6. Is the Chinese tendency to conform to styles of clothing actually much different from ours? How is it different? How about the conformity of political thinking?

7. Will the Western world have to impose some of the same controls as China on its people in twenty-five years when our population gets much bigger and our resources much less? Suppression of individual fulfillment for the good of the group? Will we also have to stop having dogs and cats as pets, because they consume food that should be for humans? Assignment of jobs? Compulsory periods of work to grow food after high school graduation?

8. What are/were China's approaches to solving the following problems and can China's solutions give us clues to solving our own: medical care to indigents, inflation, mental illness, orphans, the elderly, drug addiction, venereal diseases, energy shortages, crime, unemployment, prostitution, political corruption, and garbage disposal?

6. Is the Chinese lack of interest in sex and sex-related activities, particularly among young people, and our own obsession with sex, the result of cultural conditioning or an inherent physiological difference?

7. Is it true that each commune is an economically self-sufficient entity; that if nuclear weapons destroyed Peking and some of the other cities, life could continue almost as if nothing had happened?

8. What is China losing by being such a controlled country?

ENTERTAINMENT

All movies and stage presentations are political insofar as they support the ideals of the party in power. They are educational processes aimed primarily at teaching the value of the revolution; how bad life was before, how to make it good now; self-sacrifice, self-reliance, hard work, helpfulness, thrift, perseverance, and improvisation.

One aspect of the Cultural Revolution was to make the arts support these ideals, weakened after sixteen years of the same government. To the Chinese Communist, art exists to serve the Revolution, the proletariat. Anything sentimental, frivolous, anything that smacks of hedonism, mythology, vanity—all bourgeois ways—has been eliminated or is presented as evil.

This does not mean that movies and stage shows are dull. There is a great traditional fighting scene in "Taking Tiger Mountain by Strategy," and if you like ballet, "The White Haired Girl" and "The Red Detachment of Women" have some spectacular dancing. If you find the acting too stylized, just remember that traditional Chinese theater, with exaggerated gestures, has always been stylized. The inspirational endings remind me of a lot of old American movies.

In 1973, I found an "opera" performance to be a choir in gray Mao suits alternating with ballet selections on the Korean War. The songs were based on statements made by Chairman Mao. I did not find anything political about acrobatic performances, but that may be because I do not understand that much Chinese. Acrobats are delightful—balancing acts, jugglers, bird imitators, a great deal of fun. *Wu shu* performances feature the traditional martial arts—no guns, just swords, spears, chains, staves, and bare hands—the only weapons the masses had. On stage, it is performed with much rhythm and beauty, and exciting acrobatics.

PLACES TO VISIT

If superimposed on North America, China would reach from south of Cuba almost to James Bay—it is so vast. Don't expect it to be homogeneous. Some parts are richer, more fertile than others. Some parts grow rice; others wheat.

Its people are ethnically diverse. Most are Hans, but in the bordering areas you have tribal groups such as the Miao, Yi, Tai, and Tibetans.

Foreigners are allowed to visit many cities and their environs, and I hope you also can visit the different parts of the country to see the differences.

The following is a list of cities foreigners have been able to visit since the Cultural Revolution, and some of the things they saw there. Let me know if you visit others. If you want more details, look up Nagel's Guide or the books by the travelers whose names are in parentheses. The titles of their books are listed in the Bibliography. In many cases, these travelers name the people they met and give statistics about the institutions they visited. It might be helpful to compare notes if you go to the same places.

As with all place names, my spelling may be different from that of other travelers and guidebooks. For names of cities and provinces, I am using the Wade spelling with the *pin yin* in parenthesis. While you will find the *pin yin* on signs at airports and train stations, the

124

Wade spellings are more common in the West and are used in English-language geography books and maps produced by the Chinese themselves. In any case, the spelling systems all attempt to be phonetic.

I list these places to help you plan your trip. For suggested groupings of cities on your itinerary, see Sample Prices in Chapter 15.

ANSHAN (An shan)

In Liaoning (Liao ning) province, formerly Japanese-controlled Manchuria, adjacent to Korea. The only group I've heard of going there recently were Canadian workers in July 1974. In this industrial, iron ore, and coal-producing center, visitors see the biggest iron and steel works in the country, workers' housing, recreational facilities, and schools.

ANYANG (An yang)

In Honan (He nan) province north of the Yellow River is a cotton textile center and the place to stay when you visit the Red Flag Canal (see Salisbury and Dedmon). Visitors have gone to the Chengkuan People's Commune and Jentsun People's Commune to see power stations, schools, fertilizer and light bulb factories, etc. Visitors are shown scale models of the communes, with lights depicting the flow of the irrigation waters—a vivid presentation.

Anyang is an important place for excavations of Shang period tombs and the foundations of buildings. Seventeenth to eleventh century B.C. It was here that the oracle bones were found. These were the ancient means of divination by means of tortoise shells and shoulder blades of oxen.

CANTON

Known in Chinese as *Kwangchow* (Guang zhou), this is the capital of Kwangtung (Guang dong) province in south China adjacent to Hong Kong and Macao. The first waves of Chinese immigrants to North America in the late 1800s came from this area. And many European and American traders lived there, confined to a district called Shamien, an island near the People's Bridge in the vicinity of the Nan-fang Department Store and the Friendship Store. You can see relics of those colonial days—Ling Nam university founded by missionaries, now the site of Chung Shan University (Wilson, Terrill), and the old French Cathedral, built in the 1860s.

Another relic of interest especially to Overseas Chinese is the Mausoleum of the Seventy-two Martyrs at Huanghuakang, Yellow Flower Hill. The martyrs lost their lives a few months before the 1911 revolution in an abortive uprising against the Manchus. This lovely park is on the road to the zoo, and the memorial itself is a pyramid of stone blocks, on each of which is inscribed in Chinese and English that the stone was contributed by the Chinese Nationalist League in Chicago, Illinois, or Moose Jaw, Saskatchewan, or Lima, Peru, etc.

Other attractions include Yuehsiu Park near the new railway station. It has an Olympic-size swimming pool; a stadium; Chenhai Tower (built in 1380), now a ceramics museum; an artificial lake; a botanical exhibit; and statues of a Ping-Pong player and of several goats.

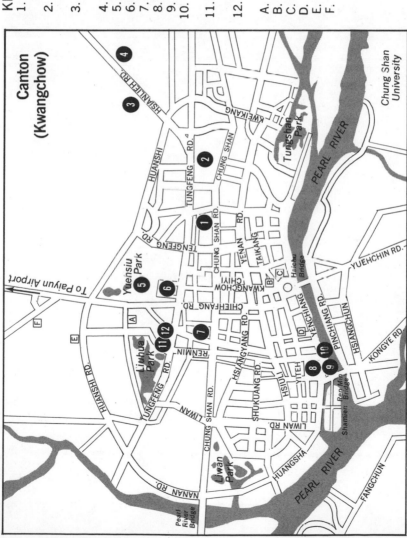

Canton (Kwangchow)

Goats have a historical connection with Canton, but no one seems to know what.

There are also the South China Botanical Gardens, some of the biggest in the country; the Memorial Gardens to the Martyrs of the Kwangchow Uprising in 1927, with its beautiful pavilions; and Kwangchow Cultural Park (tell the taxi driver Man Fa Goong Yuen), best seen after 7:00 P.M., when its several exhibit halls are open showing life-size sculptures of pre-Liberation scenes, the fishing industry, and crafts. There are also theaters, children's playgrounds, and cultural performances there.

The zoo has a good assortment of animals such as pandas, kittens (because pets are rare), bamboo-eating elephants (we were allowed to feed them), and a monkey mountain. Visitors also see the Peasant Movement Institute, founded in 1924 in a former Confucian temple, where Communist peasant cadres were trained until 1927.

The Trade Fair is housed in a building near the railway station and the Tung-fang Hotel, and you can see the fair if its dates coincide with your visit. The dates are in Chapter 15.

Visitors are also taken outside Canton to the Ping-chow People's Commune, the Tsung Hua Hot Springs (Terrill), and the Seven Star Bluff, the latter described by one visitor as "more beautiful than Hangchow."

CHANGCHUN (Chang chun)

This is the capital of Kirin (Ji lin) province in what used to be Japanese-controlled Manchuria. It is an industrial center—truck and car factory, machine-building factories, and cotton mill. It also has scientific research institutes and a film studio. It was on the itinerary of the Canadian workers' group, but I know of no one else who has gone there.

CHANGSHA (Chang sha)

Capital of Hunan (Hu nan) province north of Kwangtung, Changsha is forty miles from Shao Shan, the 1893 farmhouse birthplace of Chairman Mao, which is now a museum (Salisbury). Shao Shan is reachable by public bus. Visitors are also taken to other Mao pilgrimage spots: the Hunan First Normal School where Mao studied and later taught (Salisbury, Terrill), and Self-Cultivation University founded by Mao in 1921 but closed by the local warlord in 1923 (Terrill).

Visitors also see the Hunan Science and Engineering University and Kao Tung Ling Commune (Salisbury). Changsha is a center for trading and light and heavy industries.

CHENGCHOW (Zheng zhou)

The capital of Honan (He nan) province, a few miles south of the Yellow River, Chengchow is one of the most important cotton textile centers in the country. It is also in a wheat and sesame oil processing area. Visitors there have seen a school, hydroelectric station, live opera, and a hospital where they were given the choice of watching three simultaneous surgical operations using acupuncture anesthesia. The site of the city is 4,000 years old.

FUSHUN (Fu Shun)

In Liaoning (Liao ning) province, Fushun is frequently combined with Shenyang and Anyang on an itinerary, because they are relatively close together in China's industrial northeast. It is China's biggest coal center.

HANGCHOW (Hang zhou)

The capital of Chekiang (Zhe jiang) province (Galbraith, Wilson), Hangchow is on most itineraries because it is near Shanghai, another favorite, and because it is considered one of the most beautiful resort cities in China. It was a Sung dynasty capital (A.D. 1127–1279) and is at one end of the Grand Canal (Peking is at the other), which was begun during the Spring and Autumn Period (770–475 B.C.). Do read descriptions by Marco Polo and other travelers who saw it in its ancient glory.

Among its many attractions are West Lake (Xi hu) with its beautiful gardens, giant goldfish, the Interrupting Bridge, the Pai Chu-yi Causeway, the Three Pools that Mirror the Moon, the Su Tung-po Causeway, the Mid-Lake Pavilion, and the Two Cloud Piercing Peaks. The lake was a favorite of the Tang dynasty poet Li Po.

The luxurious-looking mansions around the lake, once owned by the rich, are now rest homes or sanatoria for working people.

Visitors have also seen the Bao Shu Pagoda, the thousand-year-old Liu He Pagoda with its panoramic view of the Qian tang River, the Ling Yin Temple with its

129

Visitors have been shown the four-mile-long double-decked bridge over the Yangtze River (Wilson, Galbraith), the Mausoleum of Sun Yat-sen where you can climb 700 steps (Wilson, Galbraith), and the Ming Tombs where one may see the same kind of stone animals which line the way to the Ming tombs north of Peking (Galbraith). There is also Hsuan Lake with its five islands; "one of the world's most charming parks," says Galbraith.

Scientist Tuzo Wilson visited the Nanking Institute of Geology and Paleontology, the Tsechin (Zi jin—Purple Mountain) Observatory with its collection of ancient astronomical instruments, and the Changlan Optical Instrument Factory.

Nanking has an excellent museum, famous for its well-exhibited collection of recently excavated objects. It is also the setting for one of China's classic novels, Wu Ching-tzu's *The Scholars.*

PEKING (Bei jing)

The capital of China, Peking is surrounded by Hopei (He bei) province on the northern fringe of the North China Plain. The essential scenic attractions are:

The **Tien An Men** (Gate of Heavenly Peace), the most famous structure in China except for the Great Wall. From its high balcony, the imperial edicts were read, and on October 1, 1949, Chairman Mao Tsetung proclaimed the People's Republic of China. Party leaders have appeared here on national days to review the parades and festivities.

In front of the gate is the 98-acre Tien An Men Square, in the center of which are monuments to the

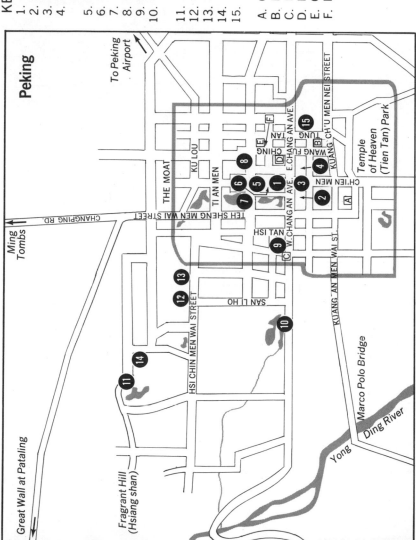

Peking

KEY

1. Tien An Men
2. Great Hall of the People
3. Monument to the People's Heros
4. Museums of Chinese History and the Chinese Revolution
5. Forbidden City and Palace Museum
6. Chung Shan Park
7. Pei hai Park
8. National Art Gallery
9. Cultural Palace of Nationalities
10. Military Museum of the Chinese People's Revolution
11. Summer Palace
12. Zoo
13. Peking Exhibition Center
14. Peking University
15. Railway station

A. Chien Men Hotel
B. Hsin Chiao Hotel
C. Nationalities Hotel
D. Peking Hotel
E. Overseas Chinese Hotel
F. Peace Hotel

To Peking Airport

Ming Tombs

Great Wall at Pataling

Fragrant Hill (Hsiang shan)

CHANGPING RD.

THE MOAT

KU LOU

TI AN MEN

TIEH SHENG MEN WAI STREET

HSI CHIN MEN WAI STREET

SAN LI HO

HSI TAN

W. CHANG AN AVE.

E. CHANG AN AVE.

TUNG CHING TAN

WANG FU CHING

KUANG CH'U MEN NEI STREET

CHIEN MEN

KUANG AN MEN WAI ST.

Temple of Heaven (Tien Tan) Park

Marco Polo Bridge

Yong

Ding River

People's Heroes. The **Great Hall of the People** is on the right. This is the site of the People's Congresses, and also state banquets and receptions.

On the left is the Museum of Chinese History and the Museum of the Chinese Revolution, which were closed during the Cultural Revolution. The big outdoor portraits are of Stalin, Marx, Engels, and Lenin.

Behind the Tien An Men is **Chung Shan Park**, named after Dr. Sun Yat-sen (whose memorial name is Chung Shan) and full of exquisite pavilions, trees, bandstands, and caldrons of goldfish. Behind this is the **Forbidden City**, the former home and audience halls of the imperial family, now open so that everyone can see the achievements of the workers who built it. Only a number of halls are occupied by the **Palace Museum**, showing personal treasures of the imperial family. In other halls objects excavated during the Cultural Revolution are on display.

To walk leisurely from one end of the Forbidden City to the other takes about twenty minutes. But to explore pavilions, many of which are full of priceless ivories, jades, porcelains, and paintings; to sit and enjoy the tranquillity of its gardens; to look into the private chambers of the Empress Dowager; to look for the servants' quarters and the wells where servants and even some members of the imperial family committed suicide—this takes a full day—some would say a week. And there is a snack bar, so you won't starve while you do it.

If it is open, you can get a good bird's eye view of the Forbidden City from Coal Hill, which is across the road out of the rear gate.

The **Temple of Heaven** (Tien Tan) is set in the middle of a vast park. Be sure you have your taxi wait for you, as your chances of finding transportation without a long walk are very slight.

Give yourself at least twenty minutes for a quick look, an hour for a more thorough tour. There are actually four main structures here—the Hall of Prayer for Good Harvests to the north, the Imperial Vault of Heaven and nearby echo wall to the south, and beyond that, the circular Sacrificial Altar. Near the west gate is the Hall of Fasting.

The temple was used a couple of times a year by the emperor, who, bearing all the sins of the Chinese people, humbled himself before Heaven and performed the rituals calculated to bring good harvests. There is a snack bar here, too.

The **Summer Palace** (Yiheyuan). Seven miles northwest of Peking, this was built in the eighteenth century and used last by the Empress Dowager who squandered money on it meant for the reconstruction of the Chinese navy. This is a vast estate with many pavilions, palaces, a library, statues, gardens, shrines, and temples. It takes at least forty-five minutes to walk leisurely from one end to the other and at least three or four hours to explore. Do see the famous "marble boat" and take a ride in a small boat on Kunming Lake. There is a good restaurant here.

The **Great Wall** and the **Ming Tombs** are usually combined because they are both north of Peking and can be "done" in four hours by taxi if you don't linger. Normally it takes a full day with lunch at the Great Wall. There is a snack bar, but better take a lunch from the hotel.

The portion of the Great Wall open to visitors is at

Pataling, accessible by train if you wish, though the Ming Tombs are not. Built to protect China from invasions, the Wall has been estimated at 1,500 to 4,000 miles long, depending on what you measure. It winds and has a lot of offshoots, some of them running parallel. You can walk several hundred feet in either direction, until you come to a sign that says to go no farther.

On the road to the Ming Tombs, you will pass a row of guardian animals, called the Sacred Way. If you want to stop for photographs of yourself on a horse or camel, just ask your guide. There is a museum in one tomb with a display of what was found buried there.

If you have more than three days for historic sites, then also ask for:

Pei hai Park (if it has been reopened since the Cultural Revolution) with its White Dagoba built in 1651, its famous Screen of the Nine Dragons, its lake, and the former palace of Kublai Khan. Its charm lies also in the old men who air their birds there, happy school children, *tai chi chuan* addicts, and fishermen.

Fragrant Hill (Hsiang shan), a 384-acre park in the Western Hills, formerly a hunting palace for many emperors. It contains pavilions and the Glazed Pagoda, but its beauty lies in its scenery, especially in the autumn.

Not far from the park is the fifteen-foot bronze sleeping Buddha, believed to be the largest of its kind in China.

Visitors have also taken in:

The No. 2 Cotton Textile Mill (Galbraith, Wilson); No. 3 Cotton Textile Plant (Salisbury); Peking Arts and Crafts Factory—ivory and jade carving, bottle painting, and cloisonné (Galston, Galbraith, Terrill); Tang-shan pottery center southeast of Peking (Galston); Beijing Yuetan, the No. 1 Semiconductor Equipment Factory (Galston); a padlock factory; No. 1 Transistor Equipment Factory of Western Peking (Salisbury); and the Heavy Generator Factory (Salisbury).

The No. 3 Affiliated Hospital of Peking Medical College, Capital Hospital (formerly Anti-Imperialism Hospital—Dedmon was a patient), and Friendship Hospital (Dedmon).

Peking University (Galston, Galbraith, Dedmon, Wilson) and Tsinghua University, China's leading technical and engineering school and a center of activity during the Cultural Revolution (Salisbury, Galston, and Terrill). Peking University is on the site of the former American school, Yenching University.

Research institutes of the Academy of Science (Galston, botanical and microbiological; and Wilson, geophysics and paleoanthropology).

School for Deaf-Mutes (Galston), Physical Education College (Terrill), and 31st Middle School (Salisbury).

East Is Red May 7 School (twenty miles southwest of Peking—Dedmon).

Nearby communes such as the Marco Polo Bridge (Lukouchiao) Commune (Galston lived there), Red Star Commune, and Double Bridge Commune, also known as the China-Cuba Friendship People's Commune where they raise 40,000 Peking ducks (Salisbury). If you're going to the first, ask about the Marco Polo Bridge incident of July 7, 1937, which set off the Japanese-Chinese war.

The Cultural Palace of the Nationalities, a museum depicting the terrible things done in the past to the ethnic minorities, as well as a place devoted now to the preservation of their cultures.

If they have reopened since the Cultural Revolution, see the Museums of Chinese History and the Chinese Revolution, the Military Museum of the Chinese People's Revolution, and the Museum of Chinese Art.

The underground air raid tunnels (Bergen) and Peking Subway (Salisbury); the Peking Opera House (Galston), Edgar Snow's grave, a neighborhood health clinic, the Peking Zoo (pandas, the U.S. musk oxen, puppy dogs—ask about the Canadian beavers), markets, Hsinhua News Agency, and the Wang Fu Ching department store.

If you want to play tennis, table tennis, pool, or bridge, or to swim, there's the air-conditioned International Club. You need your passport to get in.

You really need a month to explore Peking; it is full of immense gates, bridges, old temples, pagodas, churches, and palaces; it is the center—a capital city of a political ideology, a world in many ways different from the rest of mankind, in many ways the same.

SHANGHAI (Shang hai)

Bordering on Kiangsu (Jiang Su) and Chekiang (Zhe jiang) provinces, Shanghai is China's largest port, a great commercial and industrial city with universities and scientific institutes. It is at the mouth of the Yangtze River and parts of it are bisected by the Whangpoo (Huang pu) River.

As you ride around the city, you will see some European-style and Japanese-style houses and buildings. Many foreign countries ruled their own enclaves here before 1940. The foreigners' houses are now divided up into apartments, and you may see one of the large mansions used as a children's palace. The large buildings built by the foreigners along the Bund are now government offices, hotels, and the Seamen's Club.

There is a permanent industrial exhibition (Galbraith) if you like industrial exhibitions, and the Lu Hsun (Lu Xun) Memorial Park with the grave of China's foremost writer and the Lu Hsun Museum, but not much else in the way of tourist-type attractions. But Shanghai does have a very good museum rich in neolithic pottery, Bronze Age ritual vessals, and Chinese paintings.

Perhaps the nicest thing I can say is that Shanghai is close to Soochow, Nanking, and Hangchow. And the communes here are among the richest in China.

Visitors have also seen:

Futan University (Salisbury, Terrill), Workers' University (Dedmon), and Tung-chi University (Wilson).

Research institutes of the Chinese Academy of Science (astronomical and seismographical—Wilson); also institutes of plant physiology and biochemistry.

Malu People's Commune (Galston, Terrill), Machow People's Commune, Hsu Hang People's Commune (Galbraith), and Rainbow Bridge People's Commune.

A bus factory, electric machinery manufacturing plant, machine tools factory (Galbraith), diesel engine factory, toy factory, and an automobile and truck factory (Dedmon).

Hoa Shan Hospital (Galbraith) and No. 6 People's Hospital (where rejoining severed limbs is a specialty).

The Shanghai Opera House, Ching An Children's Palace (Galston), Tsao Yang No. 2 Middle School (Galbraith), a workers' palace, the docks (Bergen), the Tien Shan Workers' Village (Dedmon), Minghai Industrial

Shanghai

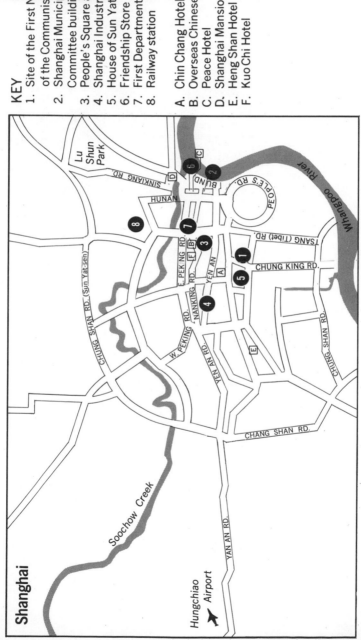

KEY

1. Site of the First National Congress of the Communist Party of China
2. Shanghai Municipal Revolutionary Committee building
3. People's Square and People's Park
4. Shanghai Industrial Exhibition
5. House of Sun Yat-sen
6. Friendship Store
7. First Department Store
8. Railway station

A. Chin Chang Hotel
B. Overseas Chinese Hotel
C. Peace Hotel
D. Shanghai Mansions
E. Heng Shan Hotel
F. Kuo Chi Hotel

Town, the Wen Hui Pao newspaper office (Salisbury), and the site of the First National Congress of the Communist Party of China.

Visitors have had sessions on "social transformation," such as how China overcame drug addiction, and on city problems such as housing, pollution, crime, and population (Dedmon).

Don't forget about shopping. The Friendship Store on the site of the former British consulate is quite large, and the Shanghai shops in general have a lot more variety than those in other parts of China.

SHENYANG (Shen Yang)

Formerly Mukden, the capital of Liaoning province bordering on Korea, Shenyang is the biggest industrial city of this region, which was formerly Japanese-held Manchuria. It was also the capital of the Manchu dynasty.

It is a cultural center with institutions of higher learning and research institutes, as well as the home base of the Shenyang Acrobats who toured the U.S. and Canada in 1973.

SHIHCHIACHUANG (Shi jia zhuang)

Shihchiachuang, south of Peking in Hopei (He bei) province, is a stop for many Canadian visitors because it has a hospital dedicated to Dr. Norman Bethune, the Canadian doctor who gave his life tending Communist army wounded in the Sino-Japanese War. He is held up in all China as a hero to be emulated.

Visitors see the hospital, its medicinal herb gardens,

139

the Bethune Exhibition Hall and Museum, and the Martyrs' Mausoleum and Memorial Park. The city is a textile center.

SIAN (Xi an)

Capital of Shensi (Shân xi) province, Sian was the capital of eleven dynasties over a period of a thousand years, when it was known as Changan. These included the Han, Sui, and Tang dynasties. It also was the site of a neolithic matriarchal society 6,000 years ago (so why don't *you* ask them why they think it was matriarchal?), and is rich in historical remains, palaces, temples, gates, and mosques.

Today it is an industrial center, specializing in textiles, machine building, and chemicals, but a lot of the ancient relics remain.

The neolithic remains can be seen in the Panpo Village Museum (Wilson), and the later 4,000 years of history can be seen in the Shensi Provincial Museum, housed in a former Confucian temple.

An interesting bit of modern history can be seen at the Huaching Hot Springs. Here a plaque marks the spot where the Nationalist leader Chiang Kai-shek was kidnapped in 1936, in a more or less successful effort to force him to cooperate with the Communists in the fight against the Japanese.

Visitors have interviewed the Shensi Acrobatic Company (Terrill), the Red Guard Art Troup (Terrill), and the Shensi Song and Dance Ensemble (Salisbury).

They have seen the Shuang Wang Commune (Dedmon), Textile Plant No. 4, No. 1 Northwest Cotton Textile Mill, Northwestern University (Wilson), Communications (Chiao Tung) University (Terrill), a factory for porcelain insulators (Wilson), and a handicraft factory making pottery, screens, and seashell pictures.

It is hard to miss the Wild Goose Pagoda or the imposing fourteenth-century Ming Bell Tower, once used as a jail for Communists.

SOOCHOW (Su Zhou)

Along with Hangchow, Soochow is considered one of the two most beautiful cities of China. With its canals and curved bridges, Soochow on Taihu Lake is the Venice of China, but it is also famous for its temples and extraordinary gardens. Musts are the pagoda on Huchiu (Tiger) Hill, the Hanshan Temple, Paotai Bridge, Shihhu Lake, the Chocheng Garden, the Lion Forest, and the Tsanglang Pavilion.

Soochow was the capital of the Wu dynasty in the sixth century and, like Hangchow, is also famous for its silk industry.

If you are a connoisseur of gardens, do see the ones in Soochow.

TIENTSIN (Tian jin)

An hour by train east of Peking, Tientsin is the capital of Hopei (He bei) province, and an educational, commercial, and manufacturing center: iron and steel, cotton, machinery, chemicals, and salt. Its proximity to the Pohai Sea has made it a fishing center, and it is near Hsinkang, now one of the world's biggest artificial harbors. Tientsin dates from the Sung dynasty, and like Shanghai it was divided into foreign concessions in the 1800s and early 1900s.

TSINAN (Ji nan)

Capital of Shantung (Shan dong), Tsinan is a city of springs, the most famous of which are the bubbling Pao Tu Well and the Black Tiger Well, the latter actually a miniature waterfall. There are seventy-two springs and a small lake.

It is also an industrial center with cotton mills, and iron and steel and machine-building plants, especially for making diesel engines. And there are several institutions of higher learning. The city is on a 3,000-year-old site.

WUHAN (Wu han)

Wuhan, capital of Hupeh (Hu bei) province, is really three cities—Hankow (Han kou), Hanyang, and Wuchang, separated by the Yangtze and Hanshui Rivers. Chairman Mao made his famous swim there in 1966.

At Wuchang on October 10, 1911, the first victory of the Sun Yat-sen Revolution took place, although Sun himself was absent. The site can be seen on Shouyi Road, marked by a bronze statue of Dr. Sun.

Visitors have seen the Wuhan Iron and Steel Works (Salisbury), which is second in China only to the Anshan works; the two-decker bridge over the Yangtze, completed in 1957; Kao Tang Ling People's Commune (Salisbury), and "China's finest acrobats" (Terrill).

The city itself is almost 2,000 years old, an ancient state capital. European nations also had concessions there. The communists led a successful strike there in

1921, and Chairman Mao directed the Peasant Movement Institute there after 1927.

WUSIH (Wu xi)

Wusih, in Kiangsu (Jiang su) province is an industrial and resort city straddling the Grand Canal on the northern bank of Lake Taihu, one of China's largest lakes. It is a silk-producing center, and the hills around it are filled with mulberry trees. Visitors have seen the gardens and temples, some 1,500 years old, and their springs, as well as the Ho Lan Production Brigade, and the Clay and Plaster Figures Factory (Terrill).

YENAN (Yan An)

In northern Shensi (Shân xi), Yenan is the place where Mao Tsetung and his army established their capital after the Long March, in 1937. The March took a year and covered 5,000 to 8,000 miles (accounts differ) from Kiangsi and Fukien provinces, an extraordinary feat of human ingenuity and endurance involving about 700,000 soldiers. Many of the marchers were killed by the pursuing Nationalists. Most of China's leaders today are veterans of the Long March.

In Yenan, Chairman Mao and his men consolidated their plans for taking control and governing China. Visitors (Salisbury, Wilson, Terrill) can see the caves where Mao studied, taught, and wrote, the meeting room of the Political Bureau, and the anti-Japanese University.

Visitors are also taken to the Liu Ling (Willow

143

Grove) Commune (Salisbury, Wilson), where Jan Myrdal and Gun Kessle researched their *Report from a Chinese Village* and *China: the Revolution Continued.*

You can't miss the famous pagoda that is synonymous with Yenan and appears on most postcards of the city. It stands on Chaling Hill above the city.

Plane service to Yenan is not frequent, and visitors sometimes drive from Sian to Yenan. If you do, ask your guide if you can see the memorial to the legendary Yellow Emperor at Huangling (Terrill), halfway in between.

13
Two Visits to China

CANADIAN STUDENTS

The following are details of a visit by students from the Downsview Secondary School, Downsview, Ontario, to China in 1973:

1. Following suggestion to visit China by a group of students, a committee of students and faculty advisers drew up plans for such a visit, selection of students, dates of visit, orientation, itinerary in China, and follow-up activities.

2. Received "approval in principle" from school board.

3. Sounded out Department of External Affairs, Canadian government, which suggested they contact the Chinese embassy in Ottawa.

4. On October 1, 1972, representatives of the committee called Ottawa and later presented their proposal to the Chinese embassy in person. Embassy officials suggested they write directly to Luxingshe in Peking.

This was done the same month, with a follow-up letter about six weeks later.

5. December 25, 1972: Letter from Luxingshe acknowledging their two letters and welcoming them to visit China in May-June, 1973, a year earlier than they had requested. From then on, all correspondence was with Peking, with replies from China taking two or three weeks. Copies of the committee's correspondence were sent to the Chinese Embassy in Ottawa.

6. Furious campaign starts to raise $35,000 for the trip (see Costs in Chapter 3). The last funds were committed approximately two weeks before departure.

7. Student Selection: chose thirty (five alternates) for the twenty-five places. The number was the committee's choice because it was within their financial considerations, and because it had heard Luxingshe preferred this number.

Criteria for choosing students: sixteen years and older, above-average academic achievement, approval by staff, ability to relate experiences upon return to Downsview, diverse cultural backgrounds representative of their community, representative selections of students with extracurricular and/or out-of-school interests in areas such as athletics, music, drama, art.

8. February 1973: Brief resumés on each student sent to Peking for visa application—age, country of birth, subjects studied, political affiliation, country of birth of parents. This list was approved as presented in March.

9. Six weeks of orientation for participants twice a week after normal school day.

10. May to June 1973: Visit to China approximately three weeks. Group visited: Canton, Peking, Shihchiachuang, Nanking, Shanghai and Hangchow; elementary and middle schools; a university; a hospital (watched

three operations); communes in three different geographical regions; heavy and light industries, including craft centers; youth palaces; sports complexes; Palace of Minorities; School for Minorities (Peking), and a silk factory.

Spent one very worthwhile afternoon in Shanghai in groups of three or four with interpreters, visiting families in their apartment homes. Eight different Chinese families were involved. This was repeated again in a rural setting a couple of times.

Most of their requests were granted. Those that weren't were (1) live in a commune for three-four days; (2) ride bicycles through the streets of Peking; (3) visit Inner Mongolia or another autonomous region.

11. General impressions: "An experience of a lifetime for everyone. Probably the most exciting educational experience in my fifteen years as a teacher. At the first reunion last week in Toronto, all were keenly interested in the possibilities of a return visit."

From a climatic view, dates were well chosen.

12. Recommendations for other groups: appear sincere, have a desire to learn and have well defined objectives. It might help to have a follow-up program, and carry it through.

Says one staff adviser, Ken Woods: "At no time did we present ourselves as a left- or right-leaning group, nor did our hosts at any time engage in direct, political indoctrination.

"We did feel that Luxingshe went out of its way to help and assist us in every way possible. They are most courteous and every effort appeared to be made to meet our requests."

13. Follow-up: Students have written an anecdotal report and worked on a more formal report with slides,

pictures, tapes, and a movie for use by other schools. Xerox of Canada has a thirty-minute film on the trip which has been shown locally on television.

The students have made a series of displays for public libraries and are committed to work for the next twelve months with the school board, the provincial ministry of education, and the Ontario Institute for Studies in Education to prepare comprehensive study materials on China to be available to all schools in Ontario.

Copies of these reports for educational use in Ontario can be obtained from Ms. Carol Geddis, China Studies Committee, Downsview Secondary School, 7 Hawksdale Road, Downsview, Ontario, Canada.

AN "OLD CHINA HAND'S" EXPERIENCES IN CHINA

(See Chapter 2.)

"When we got to my China birthplace, our guide asked if there was anyone we wanted to see. I gave him a list of old friends and, by staying up half the night, he located them all. I had understood from a Chinese businessman in Hong Kong that I should invite the people I wanted to see to dinner at the hotel. So I asked our guide to do this and he arranged for their transportation and a magnificent feast for six guests with three kinds of wine (which we hadn't requested). We didn't ask our interpreter to join us, partly because most of our friends spoke English, and we could use some Mandarin for those who didn't. Most importantly, however, we felt they might feel more relaxed if no 'official' person was present.

"It was a strange gathering—good old friends who were obviously glad to see us but who asked no personal questions about us or our parents who had lived there as teachers twenty years. Perhaps if we had met them separately and had had more time with them, we would have been able to talk more easily.

"In most places in China, we were met with cordiality and patience and told how bad things had been before the Liberation. But on my home turf, 'the bad old days' were conspicuous because no one mentioned them and yet, while everyone was correctly hospitable, and answered all the questions we felt free to ask, our reception was decidedly cooler. At one point, in the hospital where I was born, permission to take pictures was given only reluctantly. Though others had tried, I was the first non-Chinese foreigner connected with my parents' college who had been allowed to return.

"For others going, I would also suggest that if you enjoyed any food or place particularly when you were there before, request it and say why. That gives validity to your visit and gives Luxingshe the pleasure of giving you something they know you like. Expect to be isolated from the Chinese population in travel, lodging, and eating accommodations.

"Don't expect a grand welcome on your home turf and be grateful, and show it, for what you do get."

14
Milestones in Chinese History

THE IMPERIAL DYNASTIES

Early dates are approximate since authorities disagree, but the following will give you some guidelines:

1766–1123 B.C.	Shang or Yin
1122–256 B.C.	Chou
480–221 B.C.	Warring States
221–207 B.C.	Ch'in—China unified for the first time
206 B.C.—220 A.D.	Han
221–589	Six Dynasties
589–618	Sui
618–906	T'ang
907–960	Five Dynasties and Ten States
960–1279	Sung
1280–1368	Yuan or Mongol
1368–1644	Ming
1644–1911	Ching or Manchu

CONTACT WITH THE WEST AND MODERN CHINA

1275–92 Marco Polo serves in the court of Kublai Khan.

1583 First Christian missionaries, Matteo Ricci and Michael Ruggieri, Society of Jesus.

1839–42 The Opium War. China's defeat by Britain leads to unequal treaties that force China, among other things, reluctantly to accept the importation of opium.

1851–64 T'ai Ping Rebellion against the Manchus, led by a Christian-inspired Cantonese. An army of poor peasants establish the T'ai Ping capital at Nanking for eleven years.

1856–60 Second Anglo-Chinese War and more unequal treaties—the roots of much of the anti-foreign feelings of China today and of her desire to be self-sufficient.

1894 Sino-Japanese War. Japan takes Formosa and the Liaoning peninsula.

1899 "Open Door" Notes on China, whereby the U.S. receives assurances from the other foreign powers with designs on China that they will not cut up China into colonies—that all nations will be free to trade with China.

1900 Boxer Rebellion. A reaction, encouraged by the Empress Dowager, against the increasing foreign domination of China, resulting in attacks on all foreigners and Chinese Christians. The foreign powers react by capturing Peking on August 14, 1900, sacking the capital and forcing another humiliating treaty on the Chinese.

1911 Chinese Revolution begins against the Manchu emperors.

1912 Establishment of the Republic of China.

1919 Student demonstrations of May 4, 1919, against the Versailles Treaty mark the beginning of the national and cultural upsurge known as the May Fourth Movement, which has parallels with the Cultural Revolution.

1921 Founding of the Chinese Communist Party on July 1 in Shanghai.

1925 Death of Dr. Sun Yat-sen in Peking.

1926 Northern Expedition. Nationalist army led by Chiang Kai-shek marches north in an attempt to unify the country, which is controlled by the warlords.

1927 April 12. Purge of Communists in Shanghai by Chiang.

1931 Japanese take over Manchuria and set up puppet government headed by Pu-yi, the last of the Manchu rulers.

1931 Mao Tsetung proclaims Chinese Soviet Republic in Kiangsi province.

1934–35 The Long March. Communists retreat to northern Shensi province and eventually establish their capital at Yenan in 1937.

1936 Sian Incident. Chiang Kai-shek kidnapped at Huaching Hot Spring and forced into a wartime coalition with the Communists against the Japanese.

1937 July 7. Marco Polo Bridge Incident. Killing of Japanese soldiers near Peking sets off the 1937–45 war between China and Japan. Japan later occupies most urban areas.

1945 Japanese surrender. Chinese civil war continues in earnest.

1949 Communist victory.

PEOPLE'S REPUBLIC OF CHINA

1950 Land reform—land to the tiller.

1950 Korean War. China joins North Korea in fight against United Nations and South Korean forces.

1953 Collectivization of farms begins.

1956–57 One Hundred Flowers Movement; free expressions of opinion temporarily encouraged.

1958 Great Leap Forward—a mobilization of the Chinese people to increase economic production including citizen efforts to make backyard steel furnaces to smelt any scrap iron they could collect; communes established.

1959–62 Period of extreme economic difficulties due largely to natural calamities.

1960 Break with Russia.

1964 First Chinese atomic bomb.

1966–69 Cultural Revolution.

1968 Liu Shao-chi deposed as president.

1969 Border clashes with Soviet Union.

1971 U.S. Ping-Pong team visits China.
Lin Piao killed in plane crash.
Canada and China restore diplomatic relations.
People's Republic of China takes her seat in the United Nations.

1972 President Nixon visits China.

1973 Diplomatic missions established in Peking and Washington.

1973–74 Campaign criticizing Lin Piao and Confucius.

15
Helpful Information

OFFICIAL CHINESE HOLIDAYS

January 1	New Year's Day
January or February	Spring Festival or Chinese New Year (three days), depending on lunar calendar.
May 1	Labor Day
October 1 and 2	National Days celebrating the founding of the People's Republic of China in 1949.

TEMPERATURES

China uses Centigrade. To convert Fahrenheit into Centigrade, first subtract 32, then take 5/9 of the remainder. To convert Centigrade into Fahrenheit, first multiply by 9/5 and add 32.

WEIGHTS AND MEASURES

China uses both the metric system and the Chinese system.

1 gung-jin (kilogram)	= 2.2 pounds
1 jin or gun (catty)	= 1.33 pounds
	= .604 kilograms
1 dan (picul) = 100 catties	= 133 pounds or 60.47 kilograms
1 gung li (metric mile)	= .6 mile = 1 kilometer
1 li (Chinese mile)	= .3106 mile = ½ kilometer
1 ch'ek (meter)	= 39.37 inches
1 mou	= .1647 acres

ELECTRICITY

China uses a 220-volt system, so unless your electric razor can be adapted, take a nonelectric variety. You may also have problems with your plugs fitting Chinese sockets, which are three-holed.

CANTON TRADE FAIR DATES

(Kwangchow Export Commodities Fair) April 15 to May 15, October 15 to November 15, every year.

SAMPLE PRICES

While prices for Chinese citizens have remained relatively constant, prices affecting foreign travelers have risen in the last few years and will probably continue to

155

rise. These prices will merely give you some idea of what to expect. The rate between the Chinese *yuan* (¥) and foreign currency also fluctuates. An easy means of calculation is to divide the number of yuan by 2 to get either Canadian or U.S. dollars, or multiply your dollars by 2 to get the approximate yuan equivalent.

As of May 1974, Tung-fang Hotel, Canton: U.S.$9 a day and up for a single room and private bath. Adequate and simple meals U.S.$1 to $3 at the hotel. Elsewhere budget more if you want Peking duck and suckling pig, less if you eat only noodles. Telephone call from Canton to the United States, U.S.$18.50 for the first three minutes, plus U.S. $5.00 for each additional minute. Hiring a taxi for a full day's sight-seeing around Canton, about $18.

As of August 1973, Overseas Chinese Mansion, Canton: Bed in room shared with two other people, U.S.$3; twin beds and private bath, U.S.$20 (2 people); suite, U.S. $32. Eighteen-day Overseas Chinese group tour to Wuhan, Peking, Tientsin, Nanking, Soochow, Hangchow, and Shanghai, U.S.$376 per person, for all expenses. As of March 1974, Hong Kong to Canton first-class, train, round-trip U.S.$36.60; Canton to Shanghai round-trip flight, U.S.$150; Peking to Shanghai, one-way flight, U.S.$75; Peking to Sian, one-way flight, U.S.$66.

In 1974, Travel Unlimited was quoting U.S.$20 per person per day for hotels, meals, guide/interpreter, plus about U.S.$200 per person for transportation inside China. It offered a 21-day trip from Vancouver, 14 days of which were spent in six Chinese cities, the rest in Hong Kong; all-inclusive for Can$1,475.

In 1974, one U.S. travel agency was offering a group tour of twenty-four days from Vancouver for U.S.$1,706, taking in Peking, Shanghai, Hangchow, and Canton.

To sum up, I suggest you budget roughly for expenses in China, calculating slightly more to take inflation into account:

U.S.$25 a day minimum for foreign businessmen to the trade fair in Canton.

U.S.$50 a day for Foreign Friends, all-inclusive group tour of several Chinese cities.

U.S.$25 a day for Overseas Chinese all-inclusive group tour of several Chinese cities.

U.S.$6 a day for Overseas Chinese staying at the cheapest rates in Overseas Chinese hotels and eating in noodle and bun shops and using public buses or walking. Add cost of transportation between cities.

POPULATION FIGURES

Since there have been no population figures released on China for the last couple of decades, any figures you hear will be estimates. To give you a general idea of size, here's my guess—give or take a couple of million—of the cities over one million listed in this book. The Western estimate of China's total population is 800 million.

Shanghai	11,000,000
Peking	9,000,000
Tientsin	4,500,000
Shenyang	4,500,000
Canton	3,500,000
Wuhan	3,000,000
Nanking	2,000,000
Sian	1,500,000
Fushun	1,500,000
Changchun	1,500,000

TERMINOLOGY AND PHRASES

Visitors are bound to hear certain phrases repeated many times in conversations and government publications. The following are some of the common ones with attempts at definitions and background to help you understand.

Liberation:

The declaration of the People's Republic of China on October 1, 1949, following the defeat of the Chinese Nationalists led by Chiang Kai-shek.

The Cultural Revolution:

(Officially known as the Great Proletarian Cultural Revolution.) The Cultural Revolution started because Chairman Mao realized that Chinese revolutionary fervor was declining and China was not entirely under his control. The first shot was the publication on November 10, 1965, of an article instigated by Chairman Mao in a Shanghai daily, the *Wen Hui Pao,* attacking a play entitled *Hai Jui Dismissed from Office.* He could not get it published in Peking.

It was not until the summer of 1966, however, with the news of the activities of the Red Guards, that the world realized that something extraordinary was going on in China.

The Cultural Revolution was a political housecleaning—an attempt to return to the ideals of the Chinese Communist Revolution. Supporters of "Revisionism" as propagated by President Liu Shao-chi had been promoting, among other things, an intellectual elite and an urban base. One big quarrel was over which incentives to use to increase production: bonuses versus pure political idealism. Liu wanted bonuses.

Chairman Mao has always taught that the workers and the peasants—not the intellectuals—are the basis of the Chinese revolution. So as Mao regained his power with the help of the Red Guards and the army, many party cadres were sent to May Seventh Cadre Schools to be reeducated in the correct political thinking by learning to respect and love physical labor. Police chiefs pounded beats; doctors swept floors to help them identify with the masses and understand their problems.

Schools were closed and young people armed with the "little red book" of quotations from Mao. These Red Guards traveled around China taking part in revolutionary experiences such as the "Four Olds" Movement. In this they sought to eliminate "old ideas, old culture, old customs and old habits," and elements of foreign influence that were creeping back into the country. All of these elements were thought to create obstacles to the course of the Revolution.

Liu himself fell from power and was denounced as a traitor. The Cultural Revolution did get violent as various factions of Red Guards and workers fought with one another. Some foreigners and Overseas Chinese were physically attacked by "extremists."

While the Chinese leadership disclaims responsibility for the attacks, it does believe that the heightened political awareness of the Cultural Revolution must be kept alive or else "bad elements" will again creep into the country. This is the purpose of campaigns such as the one denouncing Lin Piao and Confucius. It is China's way of coping with the universal problem of perpetuating a revolution beyond the first generation.

Revolutionary Committees:

Revolutionary Committees have supplanted mayors, principals, and directors as leaders of city, school, factory, or commune administrations as a result of the Cultural Revolution. Their makeup might include the old mayors, principals, and directors, but they also include members of the People's Liberation Army, and representatives of the workers or students or peasants— roughly one third by the former leadership, one third by the military, and one third by the representatives of the people. Decisions are jointly made.

Criticism of Lin and Confucius:

Lin Piao is accused of trying to undermine the revolution by following the revisionist line of Liu Shao-chi and the Soviet revisionists, while at the same time disguising his true intentions by outwardly supporting Chairman Mao. After all, he did edit the "little red book."

Confucius is criticized because he supported the old slave-owning class and generally was a reactionary who wished to maintain the old oppressive society under the guise of lofty philosophical sentiments. He and Lin are likened in this respect. It should be remembered that Confucian teaching was the state orthodoxy in China from the Han Dynasty *(c.* 100 B.C.) to the twentieth century, and elements of Confucian thinking have continued in China even after Liberation.

Michelangelo Antonioni:

The Italian moviemaker Michelangelo Antonioni is

criticized because his film about China ignored modern developments like tractors and factories, and concentrated on elements of pre-Liberation life.

Class Struggle:

This refers to Chairman Mao's Marxist-derived view of society as a constant struggle between classes based on wealth and property and attitude: poor peasants, lower middle peasants, upper middle peasants, landlords, petty bourgeoisie, capitalists, etc. The aim of the class struggle is the inevitable victory of the proletariat and the establishment of true communism and a classless society.

Cultural Imperalism:

You will hear this term at schools founded by foreign missionaries, who introduced foreign textbooks, implements, and languages in a way that made many Chinese people ashamed of their own country and heritage.

Hsia Fang: (Going Down to the Country)

The policy of sending educated youth to work in the country on communes, either as peasants or school teachers or barefoot doctors, for periods from a couple of months to a lifetime, is common. The Chinese I spoke to denied that this is to avoid overpopulation in urban areas, or to give young people jobs. They said it was primarily to acquaint young people with the effect of the Revolution in the area where it has had the most impact—the countryside.

Communes:

These are groupings of several villages, and the land in between, into one economic and political unit. It is like a township and can have a population of several tens of thousands, with its own schools, medical facilities, stores, factories, etc. A commune is made up of "production brigades," which often are just new names for the old villages. Except for small, private plots where commune members grow vegetables for their own use (they can sell the surplus), all land is owned by the communes, although individual families may own their own houses. The commune might build housing for members who do not have their own houses, and provide dining facilities for those who prefer not to cook at home.

There have been attempts at urban communes, but so far there aren't any.

Cadre (kan pu):

In Chinese the term literally means "core element," and is used to describe any person who plays a full or part-time leadership role.

The National People's Congress:

This body, under the leadership of the Chinese Communist Party, is the highest organ of state power. It has met in 1954, 1959, 1964, and 1975.

Its 1,000-plus members are elected by the Army, directly by the people, or by provincial congresses, which in turn have been elected by county or municipal congresses. These in turn have been elected by rural people's commune or district congresses. It is at this lower level that most citizens vote.

Revolutionary committees are responsible to the local people's congresses. Elections on each level approve slates of candidates chosen in advance by the Communist Party.

The chairman of the National People's Congress used to be the chief of state (a position held by Liu Shao-chi from 1959 to 1968), but the Fourth People's Congress abolished the presidency. Between congresses, the country is run by the Standing Committee and the State Council elected by the People's Congress.

Politburo:

Short for Political Bureau. The Chinese Communist Party works through the state structure and various other organizations to achieve socialism and communism in China. Its highest body is the National Party Congress, elected by lower-level congresses. Its Tenth Party Congress was in August 1973.

It, in turn, elects the Central Committee of about 100 members to make decisions between congresses. The Central Committee elects various officers, committees, and bureaus of which the Political Bureau is one. Between meetings of the Central Committee, the Political Bureau and its standing committee make the decisions. Members of the Political Bureau, therefore, are the most powerful people in China.

16
Important Addresses

SOME CHINESE MISSIONS ABROAD

Telephone

Embassy of the People's Republic of China
247 Federal Highway
Watson, Canberra, A.C.T. 2602, Australia   47.5080

Embassy of the People's Republic of China
31 Portland Place
London, W.1, England   01-636-5726

Embassy of the People's Republic of China
415 St. Andrew's Street   613-234-2682
Ottawa, Canada KIN 5H3   613-234-2718

Embassy of the People's Republic of China
11, Avenue George V
Paris 8e, France   225.62.31

Embassy of the People's Republic of China
5-30 Minami Azabu, 4-chome
Minato-ku, Tokyo, Japan   446-6781

Embassy of the People's Republic of China
Kalcheggweg 10
Bern, Switzerland   447333

Liaison Office, People's Republic of China
2300 Connecticut Avenue, N.W.   202-797-8909 (visa)
Washington, D.C. 20008   202-797-9000 (chancery)

SOME FOREIGN MISSIONS IN CHINA

Embassy of Australia
41 San Li Tun
Peking   522331

British Mission
5 Kuang Hua Lu
Chien Kuo Men Wai
Peking   521961

Embassy of Canada
16 San Li Tun
Peking   521475

Embassy of France
10 San Li Tun
Peking   521331

Embassy of Japan
48 San Li Tun
Peking   522055

Embassy of Switzerland
25 Dong An Men Nan Jie
Peking   551914, 551259

Liaison Office of the United States of America
17 Guanghua Road
Peking   522033

ORGANIZATIONS IN CHINA DEALING WITH FOREIGN VISITORS

China International Travel Service (Luxingshe)
East Changan Street
Peking

Foreign Affairs Department
Academy of Sciences
Wen Ching Chieh No. 3
Peking

Foreign Affairs Department
Scientific and Technical Association
Peking

Chinese Medical Association, c/o Academy of Science
Wen Ching Chieh No. 3
Peking

All-China Sports Federation
Peking

Information Department
Ministry of Foreign Affairs, Peking

Committee for Cultural Relations with Foreign
Countries
Peking

Chinese People's Association for Friendship with
Foreign Countries
Peking

People's Institute for Foreign Affairs
Peking

COMMERCIAL ADDRESSES IN CHINA

Chinese Council for the Promotion of International
Trade
Peking

The following are at 82 Donganmen Street, Peking:

China National Cereals, Oils and Foodstuffs Import
and Export Corporation

China National Native Produce and Animal By-
Products Import and Export Corporation

China National Light Industrial Products Import and
Export Corporation

China National Textiles Import and Export
Corporation

The following are at Erligou, Xijiao, Peking:

China National Chemicals Import and Export
Corporation

China National Machinery Import and Export
Corporation

China National Metals and Minerals Import and Export Corporation

Bank of China, Head Office
San Li Ho
Peking

HONG KONG ADDRESSES

China Travel Service (H.K.)
77, Queen's Road, Central
Hong Kong   5-259121

China Travel Service (Kowloon)
27 Nathan Road, 1st floor
(entrance on Peking Road)
Kowloon, Hong Kong   3-664127

Chinese Chamber of Commerce
24 Connaught Road, Central
Hong Kong   5-228304

Bank of China
2A Des Voeux Road, Central
Hong Kong   5-234191

American Chamber of Commerce
322 Edinburgh House
Hong Kong   5-234380

U.S. Consulate
26 Garden Road
Hong Kong   5-239011

Office of the Commission for Canada
14/15 Floor
Asian House
1 Hennessy Road, P.O. Box 20264
Hong Kong   5-282422

Some Chinese Government Stores—Hong Kong

Chinese Arts and Crafts (H.K.) Ltd.
Star House, Kowloon, Hong Kong   3-674061

Chinese Merchandise Emporium Ltd.
92 Queen's Road, Central, Hong Kong   5-241051

Yue Hwa Chinese Products Emporium Ltd.
241 and 300 Nathan Road, Kowloon,
   Hong Kong   3-305311

Yue Hwa Chinese Products Emporium Ltd.
54-64 Nathan Road, Kowloon

FOREIGN ORGANIZATIONS

Helpful Generally:

(Some have organized tours to China.)

National Committee on U.S.-China Relations
777 United Nations Plaza
New York, N.Y. 10017

Committee on Scholarly Communication with the People's Republic of China
c/o National Academy of Sciences
2101 Constitution Avenue
Washington, D.C. 20418

The Guardian Independent Radical Newsweekly
33 West 17th Street
New York, N.Y. 10011

U.S.-China People's Friendship Association
Box 40503, Palisades Station, Washington, D.C. 20016;
Room 611, 41 Union Square West, New York City, N.Y.
   10003, phone 212-255-4727;
Room 502, 50 Oak Street, San Francisco, Cal. 94102,
   phone 415-863-0537;
Suite 1085, 407 S. Dearborn, Chicago, Ill. 60605, phone
   312-922-3414.

Canada-China Friendship Association
33 East Hastings Street
Vancouver, 4, B.C.

Committee for Concerned Asian Scholars
c/o Chris Gilmartin
4515 Osage Avenue
Philadelphia, Pa. 19143

Canadian Society for Asian Studies
York University
Downsview, Ont., Canada

Helpful to Businessmen:

National Council for U.S.-China Trade
1100 17th St. N.W., Suite 513
Washington, D.C. 20036

China Consultants International, Limited
3286 M St. N.W.
Washington, D.C. 20007

Sino-British Trade Council
25 Queen Anne's Gate
London, England

TRAVEL AGENCIES REPUTED TO BE ORGANIZING TOURS TO CHINA

(I don't guarantee anything, but you can try.)

For Canadians:

Travel Unlimited
166 E. Pender Street
Vancouver, B.C. V6A 1T4

Travel Unlimited
869 Main Street
Winnipeg, Manitoba, R2W 3N9

Skyline Travel Service
1148 East Georgia Street
Vancouver, B.C.

Others:

Swing Greene Travel, Inc.
24 Lewis Street
Hartford, Conn. 06103

AGENCIES ORGANIZING CHARTER
FLIGHTS TO HONG KONG

(At considerably cheaper rates than regularly scheduled airlines. Some of these are for persons of Chinese or Asian origin only. Some have three flights a week. Write for fares and to see if you qualify. Mention here does not mean endorsement. And there are others.)

Canada:

Asian American Recreation Club
444 Robson Street
Suite 114
Vancouver 3, B.C.

Centrex Travel Ltd.
228 Bloor Street West
Toronto M5S IVI, Ontario

Hong Kong Overseas Travel Services
600 Bay Street, Suite 308
Toronto, 101, Ontario

Travel Unlimited
166 East Pender Street
Vancouver, B.C. V6A 1T4

United States:

(Some have branches in Europe.)

Asian-American Recreation Club (via the Pacific)
1621 El Camino Real West
Mountain View, Cal. 94040

Eupo-Air Travel Service Ltd.
(flights from Philadelphia or New York City via
London; branches also in Montreal, London,
Amsterdam and Toronto)
5 East Broadway, 1st Floor
New York, N.Y. 10038

University Air Charter Consultants
1010 Vermont Avenue
Suite 721
Washington, D.C. 20005

TRANSLATION SERVICES

(in reformed Chinese characters)

China Consultants International, Limited
3286 M Street N.W.
Washington, D.C. 20007

China Consultants International, Limited
53, Printing House
Ice House Street
Hong Kong

17
Bibliography

GENERAL BOOKS

Heren, Louis, et al. *China's Three Thousand Years: The Story of a Great Civilization.* New York: The Macmillan Co., Inc., 1974.

Roderick, John. *What You Should Know about the People's Republic of China.* New York: The Associated Press, 1972.

Wylie, Ray, ed. *China, An Introduction for Canadians.* Toronto: Peter Martin Associates, Ltd., 1973.

FOR BUSINESS PEOPLE

The People's Republic of China—Markets for Canadian Exporters. Asia Series. Department of Industry, Trade and Commerce, Ottawa, Canada.

Trading with the People's Republic of China. Prepared by the U.S. Commerce Department, Bureau of East-West Trade, Washington, D.C.

Mobius, J. Mark, and Simmel, Gerhard F. *Trading with China.* New York: Arco Publishing Company, Inc., 1973.

Neilan, Edward, and Smith, Charles R. *The Future of the China Market.* American Enterprise Institute for Public Policy Research, Washington, D.C., and Hoover Institution on War, Revolution and Peace, Stanford University, Stanford, California, 1974.

U.S. China Business Review. Bimonthly magazine. National Council for U.S.-China Trade, Washington, D.C.

ACCOUNTS OF RECENT TRAVELERS

Bergen, Candice. "Can a Cultural Worker from Beverly Hills Find Happiness in the People's Republic of China?" *Playboy,* February 1974.

Dedmon, Emmett. *China Journal.* Chicago: Rand McNally & Company, 1973.

Galbraith, J. K. *A China Passage.* Boston: Houghton Mifflin Company, 1973.

Galston, Arthur W., with Savage, Jean S. *Daily Life in People's China.* New York: Thomas Y. Crowell, 1973.

Hsü-Balzer, Eileen, Balzer, Richard J., and Hsu, Francis L. K. *China Day by Day.* New Haven: Yale University Press, 1974.

Joseph, Richard. "Look, Mao! I'm Touring." *Esquire,* August 1974.

Salisbury, Harrison E. *To Peking—and Beyond.* New York: Quadrangle Books, Inc., and Toronto: Fitzhenry and Whiteside, Ltd., 1973.

Suyin, Han. "China—A Journey to Cassia Forest." *Travel and Leisure,* May 1974. (On Kweilin.)

Terrill, Ross. *800,000,000: The Real China.* Boston, Toronto: Little, Brown & Co., 1972.

Wilson, J. Tuzo. *Unglazed China.* New York: Saturday Review Press, and Toronto: Macmillan Co. of Canada, 1973.

BOOKS BY CLOSE FRIENDS OF CHINA

Greene, Felix. *Awakened China: The Country Americans Don't Know.* Orig. pub. 1961. Westport, Conn.: Greenwood, 1973.

———. *The Enemy: What Every American Should Know About Imperialism.* New York: Random House, 1971.

Hinton, William. *Fanshen: A Documentary of Revolution in a Chinese Village.* New York: Monthly Review Press, 1967.

———. *Hundred Day War: The Cultural Revolution at Tsinghua University.* New York: Monthly Review Press, 1972.

Myrdal, Jan, and Kessle, Gun. *Report from a Chinese Village.* New York: Random House, Inc., 1965.

———. *China: The Revolution Continued.* New York: Random House, Inc., 1971.

Snow, Edgar. *Red Star over China.* 1937. Rev. ed. 1968. New York: Grove Press, 1971.

———. *The Long Revolution.* New York: Random House, Inc., 1971.

Suyin, Han. *The Morning Deluge: Mao Tsetung and the Chinese Revolution 1893–1954.* Boston: Little, Brown & Co., 1972. For pre-Liberation background, there are also her autobiographical *The Crippled Tree* (1885–1928), *A Mortal Flower* (1928–38), and *Birdless Summer* (1938–48). New York: Bantam Books, Inc., 1972.

PERSONAL ACCOUNTS OF LIFE IN THE PEOPLE'S REPUBLIC OF CHINA

Ruo-wang, Bao, and Chelminiski, Rudolph. *Prisoner of Mao: A Survivor's Account of the State Prison System of the New China.* New York: Coward, McCann & Geoghegan, Inc., 1973, and Toronto: Longman Canada Ltd., 1973.

Chen, Jack. *A Year in Upper Felicity.* New York: The Macmillan Co., Inc., 1973, London: Collier Macmillan Publishers, Ltd. 1973, and Toronto: Collier-Macmillan, Canada, Ltd., 1973.

Ling, Ken. *The Revenge of Heaven.* New York: G. P. Putnam's Sons, 1972, and Toronto: Longmans Canada, 1972.

McCullough, Colin. *Stranger in China.* New York: William Morrow & Co., 1973.

Sewell, William. *I Stayed in China.* Cranbury, N. J.: A. S. Barnes & C., Inc., and London: George Allen & Unwin, Ltd., 1966.

SPECIALIZED BOOKS AND ARTICLES

Barnett, A. Doak. *Uncertain Passage: China's Transition to the Post-Mao Era.* Washington, D.C.: The Brookings Institution, 1974.

Bulling, Anneliese Gutkind. "Archaeological Excavations in China, 1949–66." *Expedition,* Summer 1972.

———. "Archaeological Excavations in China, 1966–71." *Expedition,* Fall 1972. (Both publications available from the University Museum, University of Pennsylvania, Philadelphia, Pa., 19104.)

Fairbank, John K. *The United States and China.* 3rd ed. Cambridge: Harvard University Press, 1971.

Sidel, Ruth. *Women and Child Care in China: A First-hand Report.* New York: Hill and Wang, Inc., 1972. (Also paperback. Baltimore: Penguin Books, Inc., 1973.)

———. and Sidel, Victor W. *Serve the People.* New York: The Josiah Macy, Jr. Foundation, 1974. (On health care.)

FOR OVERSEAS CHINESE

Chan, Candice Cynda, et al. *Going Back.* Privately printed, 1973. (Available from Resource Developments and Publications, Asian-American Studies Center, Campbell Hall, University of California, Los Angeles, Cal. 90024.)

Chan, Kei-on. "Homecoming of a Cantonese." *The University of Chicago Magazine,* Summer 1974.

Ling, Fei. "Fei Ling's Diary in China." *Bridge* Magazine, April and June 1974.

Liu, William T. "Journey to Nan-chang." *Notre Dame Magazine,* August 1973.

Louie, David. "A Chinese Commune Takes a Small Step Forward." *Los Angeles Times,* July 10, 1973; also *The Washington Post,* July 23, 1973, as "Life at China's Big River Commune."

Malloy, Ruth Lor. " 'New' China Has an Old Face." *National Observer,* May 19, 1973.

———. "A Chinese-Canadian Goes 'Home.' " *Weekend Magazine,* July 28, 1973.

Ting, Jan C. *An American in China.* New York: Warner Paperback Library, 1972.

TRAVEL BOOKS

Cail, Odile. *Fodor's Peking.* New York: David McKay Co., Inc., 1973.

Nagel's Encyclopedia-Guide China. 1973 ed. New York: Hippocrene Books, Inc.

Tao, S. C. *The Guide to China.* Hong Kong: Marco Polo Publications, 1973.

Illustrated Atlas of China. Chicago: Rand McNally & Company, 1973.

China Travel Gazette. China Travel Service (H.K.) 77, Queen's Road, Central, Hong Kong. (Free. Parts in English.)

OTHERS

Quotations from Chairman Mao Tsetung. Peking: Foreign Languages Press, 1966. (If you want to take it with you to China, be sure you do not have the edition with the forward by Lin Piao. A recent visitor who had one almost had his book taken away by a Chinese in an effort to remove the writings of the disgraced former Defense Minister.)

The People's Comic Book. trans. Endymion Wilkinson. Garden City, N.Y.: Doubleday & Co., Inc., 1973.

Burns, John. "Politics Divides Canadians at Peking Language School." Toronto *Globe and Mail,* April 26, 1974.

———. "Canadian Students in China Fascinated and Frustrated." Toronto *Globe and Mail,* April 25, 1974.

Understanding China Newsletter. PASE, 300 Lane Hall, University of Michigan, Ann Arbor, Mich. 48104.

New China Magazine. Dept. CB, U.S.-China People's Friendship Association, 41 Union Square West, Room 1228, New York, N.Y. 10003.

BEST SELECTION OF CHINA BOOKS

China Books and Periodicals, 125 Fifth Avenue, New York, N.Y. 10003; or 210 West Madison, Chicago, Ill. 60606; or 2929 Twenty-fourth St., San Francisco, Calif. 94110. Write for catalog.

You can also write directly to Guozi Shudian, China Publications Centre, P.O. Box 399, Peking. They will accept personal checks.

18
Words of Frequently Heard Songs

The Internationale

Arise, ye prisoners of starvation!
Arise, ye wretched of the earth,
For justice thunders condemnation,
A better world's in birth.
No more tradition's chains shall bind us,
Arise, ye slaves, no more enthralled!
The earth shall rise on new foundations,
We have been naught; we shall be all.
'Tis the final conflict;
Let each stand in his place,
The international working class
Shall free the human race.
'Tis the final conflict;
Let each stand in his place.
The international working class
Shall free the human race.

The East Is Red

Red is the east, rises the sun.
China has brought forth a Mao Tsetung.
For the people's happiness he works,
Hu erh hai ya,
He's the people's liberator.

Chairman Mao loves the people.
Chairman Mao, he is our guide.
To build a new China,
Hu erh hai ya,
He leads us, leads us forward.

Communist Party is like the sun,
Bringing light wherever it shines.
Where there's the Communist Party,
Hu erh hai ya,
There the people win liberation.

Sailing the Seas Depends on the Helmsman

Sailing the seas depends on the helmsman,
Life and growth depend on the sun.
Rain and dewdrops nourish the crops,
Making revolution depends on Mao Tsetung's Thought.
Fish can't leave the water, nor melons leave the vine.
The revolutionary masses can't do without the Communist Party.
Mao Tsetung's Thought is the sun that forever shines.

19
Useful Chinese Phrases

If you don't speak much Chinese, you may find these helpful. Point to the Chinese here. China has too many dialects and tones to write this in phonetics, but there is only one written language.

GENERAL

(Have someone fill in the blanks for you.)

I'm sorry, I don't speak Chinese.

很抱歉，我不会讲中文。

I speak English.

我讲英文。

My name is ———.

我名叫....

I am from ———.

我是从......来。

I am in China for ——— weeks.

我会在中国逗出....个星期。

           ——— months.

          .....个月。

This is my first visit.

这是我第一次的旅行。

And you?

你呢？

EATING

If you have a menu in English, please bring it.

要是你们有英文的菜单，请拿来給我。

Please bring me a bowl of noodle soup.

请拿一碗湯麵給我。

What do you recommend that is good but not too expensive?

请介紹一些价廉味美的菜。

What is the specialty of this restaurant?

这里有些甚么特別的菜？

Please bring me some ———·请来一盤....

beef 牛肉

chicken 雞

crab	螃蟹	deep fried	炸
duck	鴨	poached	煮
eggs	蛋	soup	湯
fish	魚	steamed	蒸
goose	鵝	roasted	燒烤
pork	猪肉	bland	清淡
shrimp	虾	salted	鹹
fruit	水果	sour	酸
vegetables	蔬菜	spicy hot	辣
fried	炒	sweet	甜

I understand Foreign Friends and Overseas Chinese do not have to give ration coupons.

据我所知,外国朋友及华侨都不须配給证的。

TAKING PICTURES

May I take a photo of you?

我能替你拍一張照片嗎?

185

I am visiting here and I would like to show my relatives at home what life is like in the new China.

我是在此旅行；我希望給我的親友看看新中國的生活。

I'm sorry, I didn't know I couldn't take photographs.

对不起，我不知道这里是不许拍照的。

May I have my camera back?

请你把我的照相机还給我。

EMERGENCIES

What is happening here?

这里发生了甚么事？

Please call a policeman and someone who speaks English and Chinese.

请替我找一位警察及一位能说中英语的同志。

Please contact the embassy of ———.

请替我联络……大使館。

Australia

澳洲

Britain

英国

Canada

加拿大

186

France

法国

Japan

日本

Switzerland

瑞士

Please contact the U.S. Liaison Office.

请替我与美国驻华联络处联络。

MEDICAL

I have a pain here.

我这里很痛。

I have diarrhea.

我瀉肚。

I have a cold.

我感冒了。

I need some medicine.

我需要一点药。

I want to see a doctor.

我想看医生。

TRAVEL

I want to take a taxi.

我想坐小汽車。

—train

火車

—airplane

飛机

—passenger boat

客船

I would like to get permission to go to———.

我想申請到 . . . . .

Can you help carry my luggage?

你能替我拿行李嗎?

Please send a car and an English-speaking guide to meet me.

请替我叫一部汽車及一位会讲
英语的导遊同志。

What time will there be a taxi or bus to take me to the airport?

甚么时候才有小汽車或公共汽車
載我到飛机场?

Where will I wait for the taxi? 我该在那里等車?

188

May I have my passport back?

请把我的護照还給我。

Overseas Chinese Travel Service

华侨旅行社

Luxingshe (China International Travel Service)

中国旅行社

Academy of Science

中国科学院

Scientific and Technical Association

中华人民共和国科技学会

Chinese Medical Association

中华医学会

MISCELLANEOUS

How much? 多少錢？

I'm sorry. 对不起。

Please. 请。

Good-bye. 再见。

Thank you. 谢谢你。

Where is the lavatory? 厕所在那里？

Men 男

Women 女

Mao. (The family surname of Chairman Mao.) 毛

one 一	twelve 十二
two 二	twenty 二十
three 三	twenty-one 二十一
four 四	thirty 三十
five 五	forty 四十
six 六	fifty 五十
seven 七	hundred 百
eight 八	thousand 千
nine 九	ten thousand 萬
ten 十	or 万
eleven 十一